PRAISE FOR DEBATING AMERICAN HISTORY

"Debating American History repositions the discipline of history as one that is rooted in discovery, investigation, and interpretation."
—Ingrid Dineen-Wimberly,
University of California, Santa Barbara

"Debating American History is an excellent replacement for a 'big assignment' in a course. It offers a way to add discussion to a class, and it is a perfect 'active learning' assignment, in a convenient package."
—Gene Rhea Tucker, Temple College

"The advantage that Debating American History has over other projects and texts currently available is that this brings a very clear and focused organization to the notion of classroom debate. The terms of the debate are clear. The books introduce students to historiography and primary sources. Most of all, the project re-envisions the way that US history should be taught. No other textbook or set of teaching materials does what these books do when taken together as the sum of their parts."
—Ian Hartman, University of Alaska

DEBATING AMERICAN HISTORY

BLACK LIBERATION FROM RECONSTRUCTION TO BLACK LIVES MATTER

DEBATING AMERICAN HISTORY

Series Editors: Joel M. Sipress, David J. Voelker

DEBATING AMERICAN HISTORY

BLACK LIBERATION FROM RECONSTRUCTION TO BLACK LIVES MATTER

Robert S. Smith
MARQUETTE UNIVERSITY

NEW YORK   OXFORD
OXFORD UNIVERSITY PRESS

Oxford University Press is a department of the University of Oxford.
It furthers the University's objective of excellence in research, scholarship,
and education by publishing worldwide. Oxford is a registered trade mark of
Oxford University Press in the UK and certain other countries.

Published in the United States of America by Oxford University Press
198 Madison Avenue, New York, NY 10016, United States of America.

© 2022 by Oxford University Press

Library of Congress Cataloging-in-Publication Data
Names: Smith, Robert Samuel, 1969- author.
Title: Black liberation from Reconstruction to Black Lives Matter / Robert
    Smith, Marquette University.
Description: New York : Oxford University Press, [2022] | Series: Debating
    American history | Includes bibliographical references and index. |
    Summary: "A higher education history text about Black liberation,
    starting with the Reconstruction Era and covering up to the Black Lives
    Matter movement"— Provided by publisher.
Identifiers: LCCN 2021003045 (print) | LCCN 2021003046 (ebook) | ISBN
    9780197583951 (paperback) | ISBN 9780197583968 (epub) | ISBN
    9780197583975
Subjects: LCSH: African Americans—Civil rights—United States. | African
    Americans—Politics and government. | African Americans—Social
    conditions. | Civil rights movements—United States—History. | United
    States—Race relations—History.
Classification: LCC E185.61 .S6535 2022 (print) | LCC E185.61 (ebook) |
    DDC 323.1196/073—dc23
LC record available at https://lccn.loc.gov/2021003045
LC ebook record available at https://lccn.loc.gov/2021003046

Printing number: 9 8 7 6 5 4 3 2 1
Printed by LSC Communications, Inc., United States of America

TABLE OF CONTENTS

LIST OF IMAGES AND FIGURES

Images

Figures

ABOUT THE AUTHOR

Rob hails from Indianapolis, IN and is the proud father of Henderson Marcellus Smith. Rob serves as the Harry G. John Professor of History and the Director of the Center for Urban Research, Teaching & Outreach at Marquette University. His research and teaching interests include US History, African American history, civil rights history, and exploring the intersections of race and law. Dr. Smith is the author of *Race, Labor & Civil Rights; Griggs v. Duke Power and the Struggle for Equal Employment Opportunity*. Prior to joining Marquette University, Rob served as the Associate Vice Chancellor for Global Inclusion & Engagement and Director of the Cultures & Communities Program at the University of Wisconsin-Milwaukee. Dr. Smith also volunteers as the resident historian for America's Black Holocaust Museum in Milwaukee, Wisconsin.

ACKNOWLEDGMENTS

It was an awesome responsibility to complete this project during 2020. Given the challenges and realities the year and moment in history provided, I owe a heartfelt thank you to the 25 million or more people who took to the streets to demand an end to police murder and police brutality. I owe the same depth of appreciation to the many grassroots organizations in city after city who called on political leadership to transfer tax-payer dollars from police budgets to human service needs such as housing and mental health support. I am also compelled to acknowledge the millions who voted in opposition to white supremacy in the various national, state and local elections of 2020. And, I am deeply thankful to all the medical experts and community-based organizations who provided tireless support to our neighbors and family members struggling to stay alive while the coronavirus wrought havoc across the country and globe, as political leadership in this country from all levels of government failed us miserably over and over.

Indeed, I do I have to offer a few particular acknowledgements to those who helped move this project along in various ways, directly and indirectly. It was tough to subsume so many important ideas into these few pages, and you all helped make that possible. Thanks to David Voelker for guiding the process while also making room for the project to mature. Thanks to Ben Linzy, Theodore "Teddy" Williams IV, Will Tchakirides, Molly Collins, Charmane Lang, Tad Maniela, Dawson Barrett, Steven Anthony, Beth Robinson, Henderson Smith, Rachel Buff, Joe Austin, Sarah Smith, Sameena Mulla, Adam Carr, Joanne Williams, Walt Lanier, Monique Liston, Lisa Lamson, Natalie Reinbold, Sharlen Moore, Nichole Yunk Todd, Tracy Benson, Mike Staples, Matt Lewis, Sean Wilson, Emilio de Torre, Mike Carriere, Marisola Xhelili Ciaccio and all the students in classes over the years for the many discussions regarding the themes, ideas and documents guiding this book. Again, thanks to each of you!

REVIEWERS

Kenneth J. Heneman, *Angelo State University*
Nancy Brown, *Purdue University*

Angela Flounory, *University of Michigan–Dearborn*
Laurie Lahey, *University of South Florida*
Gary L. Lee, *Georgia State University–Perimeter College*
Suzanne Smith, *George Mason University*
Michael Holm, *Boston University*
Patricia G. Clark, *Westminster College*
Jeff Strickland, *Montclair State University*

SERIES INTRODUCTION

Although history instruction has grown richer and more varied over the past few decades, many college-level history teachers remain wedded to the coverage model, whose overriding design principle is to cover huge swaths of history, largely through the use of textbooks and lectures. The implied rationale supporting the coverage model is that students must be exposed to a wide array of facts, narratives, and concepts in order to have the necessary background both to be effective citizens and to study history at a more advanced level—something that few students actually undertake. Although coverage-based courses often afford the opportunity for students to encounter primary sources, the imperative to cover an expansive body of material dominates these courses, and the main assessment technique, whether implemented through objective or written exams, is to require students to identify or reproduce authorized knowledge.

Unfortunately, the coverage model has been falling short of its own goals since its very inception in the late nineteenth century. Educators and policymakers have been lamenting the historical ignorance of American youth going back to at least 1917, as Stanford professor of education Sam Wineburg documented in his illuminating exposé of the history of standardized tests of historical knowledge.[1] In 2010, the *New York Times* declared that "History is American students' worst subject," basing this judgment on yet another round of abysmal standardized test scores.[2] As we have documented in our own historical research, college professors over the past century have episodically criticized the coverage model and offered alternatives. Recently, however, college-level history instructors have been forming a scholarly community to improve the teaching of the introductory course by doing research that includes rigorous analysis of student learning. A number of historians who have become involved in this discipline-based pedagogical research, known as the

---

1   Sam Wineburg, "Crazy for History," *Journal of American History* 90 (March 2004): 1401–1414.
2   Sam Dillon, "U.S. Students Remain Poor at History, Tests Show," *New York Times*, June 14, 2011, http://www.nytimes.com/2011/06/15/education/15history.html?emc=eta1&pagewanted=print.

Scholarship of Teaching and Learning (SoTL), have begun to mount a challenge to the coverage model.[3]

Not only has the coverage model often achieved disappointing results by its own standards, it also proves ineffective at helping students learn how to think historically, which has long been a stated goal of history education. As Lendol Calder argued in a seminal 2006 article, the coverage model works to "cover up" or "conceal" the nature of historical thinking.[4] The eloquent lecture or the unified textbook narrative reinforces the idea that historical knowledge consists of a relatively straightforward description of the past. Typical methods of covering content hide from students not only the process of historical research—the discovery and interpretation of sources—but also the ongoing and evolving discussions among historians about historical meaning. In short, the coverage model impedes historical thinking by obscuring the fact that history is a complex, interpretative, and argumentative discourse.

Informed by the scholarship of the processes of teaching and learning, contemporary reformers have taken direct aim at the assumption that factual and conceptual knowledge must precede more sophisticated forms of historical study. Instead, reformers stress that students must learn to think historically by doing—at a novice level—what expert historians do.[5]

With these ideas in mind, we thus propose an argument-based model for teaching the introductory history course. In the argument-based model, students participate in a contested, evidence-based discourse about the human past. In other words, students are asked to argue about history. And by arguing, students develop the dispositions and habits of mind that are central to the discipline of history.[6] As the former American Historical Association (AHA) president Kenneth Pomeranz noted in late 2013, historians should consider seeing general education history courses as valuable "not for the sake of 'general knowledge'

---

3   See Lendol Calder, "Uncoverage: Toward a Signature Pedagogy for the History Survey," *Journal of American History* 92 (March 2006): 1358–1370; Joel M. Sipress and David J. Voelker, "The End of the History Survey Course: The Rise and Fall of the Coverage Model," *Journal of American History* 97 (March 2011): 1050–1066; and Penne Restad, "American History Learned, Argued, and Agreed Upon," in *Team-Based Learning in the Social Sciences and Humanities*, ed. Michael Sweet and Larry K. Michaelson, 159–180 (Sterling, VA: Stylus, 2012). For an overview of the Scholarship of Teaching and Learning (SoTL) in history, see Joel M. Sipress and David Voelker, "From Learning History to Doing History: Beyond the Coverage Model," in *Exploring Signature Pedagogies: Approaches to Teaching Disciplinary Habits of Mind*, ed. Regan Gurung, Nancy Chick, and Aeron Haynie, 19–35 (Sterling, VA: Stylus Publishing, 2008). Note also that the International Society for the Scholarship of Teaching and Learning in History was formed in 2006. See http://www.indiana.edu/~histsotl/blog/.

4   Calder, "Uncoverage," 1362–1363.

5   For influential critiques of the "facts first" assumption, see Sam Wineburg, "Crazy for History," *Journal of American History* 90 (March 2004): 1401–1414; and Calder, "Uncoverage."

6   For discussions of argument-based courses, see Barbara E. Walvoord and John R. Breihan, "Arguing and Debating: Breihan's History Course," in Barbara E. Walvoord and Lucille P. McCarthy, *Thinking and Writing in College: A Naturalistic Study of Students in Four Disciplines* (Urbana, IL: National Council of Teachers of English, 1990), 97–143; Todd Estes, "Constructing the Syllabus: Devising a Framework for Helping Students Learn to Think Like Historians," *History Teacher* 40 (February 2007), 183–201; Joel M. Sipress, "Why Students Don't Get Evidence and What We Can Do about It," *The History Teacher* 37 (May 2004), 351–363; David J. Voelker, "Assessing Student Understanding in Introductory Courses: A Sample Strategy," *The History Teacher* 41 (August 2008): 505–518.

but for the intellectual operations you can teach."[7] Likewise, the AHA "Tuning Project" defines the discipline in a way much more consistent with an argument-based course than with the coverage model: "History is a set of evolving rules and tools that allows us to interpret the past with clarity, rigor, and an appreciation for interpretative debate. It requires evidence, sophisticated use of information, and a deliberative stance to explain change and continuity over time. As a profoundly public pursuit, history is essential to active and empathetic citizenship and requires effective communication to make the past accessible to multiple audiences. As a discipline, history entails a set of professional ethics and standards that demand peer review, citation, and toleration for the provisional nature of knowledge."[8] We have designed *Debating American History* with these values in mind.

In the coverage-based model, historical knowledge is seen as an end in itself. In the argument-based model, by contrast, the historical knowledge that students must master serves as a body of evidence to be employed in argument and debate. While the ultimate goal of the coverage approach is the development of a kind of cultural literacy, the argument-based history course seeks to develop historical modes of thinking and to encourage students to incorporate these modes of thinking into their daily lives. Particularly when housed within a broader curriculum that emphasizes engaged learning, an argument-based course prepares students to ask useful questions in the face of practical problems and challenges, whether personal, professional, or civic. Upon encountering a historical claim, such as those that frequently arise in political discussions, they will know how to ask important questions about context, evidence, and logic. In this way, the argument-based course fulfills the discipline's long-standing commitment to the cultivation of engaged and informed citizens.[9]

While there is no single correct way to structure an argument-based course, such courses do share a number of defining characteristics that drive course design.[10] In particular, argument- based courses:

1. ARE ORGANIZED AROUND SIGNIFICANT HISTORICAL QUESTIONS ABOUT WHICH HISTORIANS THEMSELVES DISAGREE.

Argument-based courses are, first and foremost, question-driven courses in which "big" historical questions (rather than simply topics or themes) provide the overall organizational structure. A "big" historical question is one about which historians themselves

---

7 Kenneth Pomeranz, "Advanced History for Beginners: Why We Should Bring What's Best about the Discipline into the Gen Ed Classroom," *Perspectives on History* (Nov. 2013), http://www.historians.org/publications-and-directories/perspectives-on-history/november-2013/advanced-history-for-beginners-why-we-should-bring-what's-best-about-the-discipline-into-the-gen-ed-classroom.

8 This definition reflects the state of the Tuning Project as of September 2013. For more information, see "AHA History Tuning Project: History Discipline Core," http://www.historians.org/teaching-and-learning/current-projects/tuning/history-discipline-core.

9 As recently as 2006, the AHA's Teaching Division reasserted the importance of history study and scholarship in the development of globally aware citizens. Patrick Manning, "Presenting History to Policy Makers: Three Position Papers," *Perspectives: The Newsmagazine of the American Historical Association* 44 (March 2006): 22–24.

10 Our approach to course design is deeply influenced by Grant Wiggins and Jay McTighe, *Understanding by Design*, 2nd ed. (Upper Saddle River, NJ: Pearson Education, 2006).

disagree and that has broad academic, intellectual, or cultural implications. Within these very broad parameters, the types of questions around which a course may be organized can vary greatly. The number of "big" questions addressed, however, must be relatively limited in number (perhaps 3–5 over the course of a typical fifteen-week semester), so that students can pursue the questions in depth.

2. SYSTEMATICALLY EXPOSE STUDENTS TO RIVAL POSITIONS ABOUT WHICH THEY MUST MAKE INFORMED JUDGMENTS.

Argument-based courses systematically expose students to rival positions about which they must form judgments. Through repeated exploration of rival positions on a series of big questions, students see historical debate modeled in way that shatters any expectation that historical knowledge is clear-cut and revealed by authority. Students are thus confronted with the inescapable necessity to engage, consider, and ultimately evaluate the merits of a variety of perspectives.

3. ASK STUDENTS TO JUDGE THE RELATIVE MERITS OF RIVAL POSITIONS ON BASIS OF HISTORICAL EVIDENCE.

To participate in historical argument, students must come to see historical argument as more than a matter of mere opinion. For this to happen, students must learn to employ evidence as the basis for evaluating historical claims. Through being repeatedly asked to judge the relative merits of rival positions on the basis of evidence, students come to see the relationship between historical evidence and historical assertions.

4. REQUIRE STUDENTS TO DEVELOP THEIR OWN POSITIONS FOR WHICH THEY MUST ARGUE ON THE BASIS OF HISTORICAL EVIDENCE.

In an argument-based course, the ultimate aspiration should be for students to bring their own voices to bear on historical discourse in a way that is thoroughly grounded in evidence. Students must therefore have the opportunity to argue for their own positions. Such positions may parallel or synthesize those of the scholars with which they have engaged in the course or they may be original. In either case, though, students must practice applying disciplinary standards of evidence.

Learning to argue about history is, above all, a process that requires students to develop new skills, dispositions, and habits of mind. Students develop these attributes through the act of arguing in a supportive environment where the instructor provides guidance and feedback. The instructor is also responsible for providing students with the background, context, and in-depth materials necessary both to fully understand and appreciate each big question and to serve as the body of evidence that forms the basis for judgments and arguments. While argument-based courses eschew any attempt to provide comprehensive coverage, they ask students to think deeply about a smaller number of historical questions, and in the process of arguing about the selected questions, students will develop significant content knowledge in the areas emphasized.

While a number of textbooks and readers in American history incorporate elements of historical argumentation, there are no published materials available that are specifically designed to support an argument-based course. *Debating American History* consists of a series of modular units, each focused on a specific topic and question in American history that will support all four characteristics of an argument-based course noted earlier. Each of the modules is designed for a roughly three- to four-week course unit. Instructors will select units that support their overall course design, perhaps incorporating one or two modules into an existing course or structuring an entire course around three to five such units. (Instructors, of course, are free to supplement the modular units with other materials of their choosing, such as additional primary documents, secondary articles, multimedia materials, and book chapters.) By focusing on a limited number of topics, students will be able to engage in in-depth historical argumentation, including consideration of multiple positions and substantial bodies of evidence.

Each unit will have the following elements:

1. THE BIG QUESTION

The unit will begin with a brief narrative introduction that will pose the central question of the unit and provide general background.

2. HISTORIANS' CONVERSATIONS

This section will establish the debate by providing two or three original essays that present distinct and competing scholarly positions on the Big Question. While these essays will make occasional reference to major scholars in the field, they are not intended to provide historiographical overviews, but rather to provide models of historical argumentation through the presentation and analysis of evidence.

3. DEBATING THE QUESTION

Each module will include a variety of materials containing evidence for students to use to evaluate the various positions and develop a position of their own. Materials may include primary source documents, images, a timeline, maps, or brief secondary sources. The specific materials will vary depending upon the nature of the question. Some modules will include detailed case studies that focus on a particular facet of the Big Question.

For example, one module that we have developed for an early American history course focuses on the following Big Question: "How were the English able to displace the thriving Powhatan people from their Chesapeake homelands in the seventeenth century?" The Historians' Conversations section includes two essays: "Position #1: The Overwhelming Advantages of the English"; and "Position #2: Strategic Mistakes of the Powhatans." The unit materials allow students to undertake a guided exploration of both Powhatan and English motivations and strategies. The materials include two case studies that serve specific pedagogical purposes. The first case study asks the question, "Did Pocahontas Rescue John Smith from Execution?" Answering this question requires grappling with the nature of primary sources and weighing additional evidence from secondary sources; given historians' confidence that Powhatan did adopt Smith during his captivity, the case study also raises important questions about Powhatan strategy. The second case study focuses on the 1622 surprise attack that the Powhatans (led by Opechancanough) launched against the

English, posing the question: "What was the Strategy behind the 1622 Powhatan Surprise Attack?" Students wrestle with a number of scholarly perspectives regarding Opechanca-nough's purpose and the effectiveness of his strategy. Overall, this unit introduces students to the use of primary sources and the process of weighing different historical interpretations. Because of Disney's 1995 film *Pocahontas*, many students begin the unit thinking that they already know about the contact between the Powhatans and the English; many of them also savor the chance to bring critical, historical thinking to bear on this subject, and doing so deepens their understanding of how American Indians responded to European colonization.

Along similar lines, the Big Question for a module on the Gilded Age asks, "Why was industrialization in the late nineteenth century accompanied by such great social and political turmoil?" The materials provided allow students to explore the labor conflicts of the period as well as the Populist revolt and to draw conclusions regarding the underlying causes of the social and political upheavals. Primary sources allow students to delve into labor conflicts from the perspectives of both the workers and management, to explore both Populist and anti-Populist perspectives. Three short case studies allow students to examine specific instances of social conflict in depth. A body of economic data from the late nineteenth century is also included.

Many history instructors, when presented with the argument-based model, find its goals to be compelling, but they fear that it is overly ambitious—that introductory-level students will be incapable of engaging in historical thinking at an acceptable level. But we must ask: how well do students learn under the coverage model? Student performance varies in an argument-based course, but it varies widely in a coverage-based course as well. In our experience, most undergraduate students are capable of achieving a basic level of competence at identifying and evaluating historical interpretations and using primary and secondary sources as evidence to make basic historical arguments. We not only have evidence of this success in the form of our own gradebooks, but we have studied our students' learning to document the success of our approach.[11] Students can indeed learn how to think like historians at a novice level, and in doing so they will gain both an appreciation for the discipline and develop a set of critical skills and dispositions that will contribute to their overall higher education. For this to happen, however, a course must be "backwards designed" to promote and develop historical thinking. As historian Lawrence Gipson (Wabash College) asked in a 1916 AHA discussion, "Will the student catch 'historical-mindedness' from his instructor like the mumps?"[12] The answer, clearly, is "no."

In addition to the modular units focused on big questions, instructors will also be provided with a brief instructors' manual, entitled "Developing an Argument-Based Course." This volume will provide instructors with guidance and advice on course development, as well as with sample in-class exercises and assessments. Additionally, each module includes an Instructor's Manual. Together, these resources will assist instructors with the process of creating an argument-based course, whether for a relatively small class at a liberal arts

---

11 See Sipress, "Why Students Don't Get Evidence," and Voelker, "Assessing Student Understanding."

12 Lawrence H. Gipson, "Method of the Elementary Course in the Small College," *The History Teacher's Magazine* 8 (April 1917), 128. (The conference discussion took place in 1916.)

college or for a large class of students at a university. These resources can be used in both face-to-face and online courses.

The purpose of *Debating American History* is to provide instructors with both the resources and strategies that they will need to design such a course. This textbook alternative leaves plenty of room for instructor flexibility, and it requires instructors to carefully choose, organize, and introduce the readings to students, as well as to coach students through the process of thinking historically, even as they deepen their knowledge and understanding of particular eras and topics.

Joel M. Sipress
Professor of History
University of Wisconsin–Superior

David Voelker
Professor of Humanities and History
University of Wisconsin–Green Bay

DEBATING AMERICAN HISTORY

BLACK LIBERATION FROM RECONSTRUCTION TO BLACK LIVES MATTER

THE BIG QUESTION

AFTER DECADES OF STRUGGLE, WAS THERE A BREAKTHROUGH IN CIVIL RIGHTS IN THE 1960S?

Recent developments compel historians to continually revisit examinations into African American struggles for full equality. A few of those developments include the election and re-election of President Barack Obama, the immediate and hostile responses to the presence of the nation's first Black president, the persistence of state violence aimed at African Americans, staggering racial disparities in education and economics, the ballooning of the incarceration and criminalization of Black people, the vitality of the Movement for Black Lives, and not the least, the readily apparent thread of White nationalism woven throughout the Trump administration and its base. In many respects, these various vectors merged in frightening ways in 2020 amid the COVID-19 pandemic, which had a disturbingly disparate impact on Black communities.

Meanwhile, scholarly discourse associated with the Long Civil Rights Movement has emerged alongside these developments, providing a unique immediacy to the historical debates. Of course, sound scholarly debate rests as much on asking insightful questions as it does on securing well-researched, well-crafted responses (essays, articles, books, op-eds . . . etc.). The task of this collection is to explore this fundamental question: *Was there a breakthrough in civil rights in the 1960s?*

This question engages the voluminous research on the Modern Civil Rights Movement of the 1950s and 1960s when, as scholars have shown, the United States witnessed powerful demands for racial equality on many fronts. Therefore, this question brings us squarely into the scholarly debates regarding the Long Civil Rights Movement. As this name suggests, we must connect the Modern Civil Rights Movement to a longer struggle or set of struggles for racial equality that includes successes leading up to the 1950s and 1960s. If a breakthrough did occur, we must also consider the lasting impacts and outcomes of the Modern Civil Rights Movement to determine whether those changes have endured. Given the deeply rooted nature of the nation's problems with race, many scholars have highlighted that gross racial inequities persist despite the upheavals of the 1950s and 1960s. Because of these realities, we are also required to consider one other question: *Is racism a permanent thread in the fabric of American society, thus requiring ongoing, potentially never-ending activism to achieve and maintain continued progress toward racial equality?*

Historians have rightfully paid substantial attention to the Modern Civil Rights Movement of the 1950s and 1960s. The "Movement" witnessed a coalescing of protest strategies and ideological underpinnings that made the eradication of Jim Crow—the system of legal segregation—possible, at least in terms of the law. The era is earmarked by demonstrative protests and philosophical arguments around civil rights that captured national and international attention. These philosophies and strategies were applied to key rights such as employment, education, voting, and housing, which collectively anchored a civil rights platform. This platform included varied approaches designed to topple Jim Crow. And it exposed the nation and world to the leadership of Dr. Martin Luther King, Jr., Ella Baker, Malcolm X, Diane Nash, Bayard Rustin, Shirley Chisolm, Dr. Angela Davis, Rep. John Lewis, and many others.

The Long Civil Rights Movement thesis has initiated scholarly debates about when the movement began, whether there have been other movements before and after the 1950s and 1960s, and where local movements and grassroots leaders fit in the history and scholarship. The Long Civil Rights Movement debate has generated a wealth of scholarship that offers comparative analyses of struggles across regions, eras, and ideologies. And the scholarly debates have produced critiques of the Long Civil Rights Movement thesis. The more expansive "Black Liberation Movement" thesis, for example, makes scholarly room for multiple movements whose philosophies and strategies diverge from those employed across the South in the battle against segregation. Two influential essays shape the foundation for this debate: Jacquelyn Dowd Hall's "The Long Civil Rights Movement and the Political Uses of the Past" and Sundiata Kieta Cha-Jua and Clarence Long's "The 'Long Movement' as Vampire: Temporal and Spatial Fallacies in Recent Black Freedom Studies."[1] The debate has made intellectual space for a richer and more complicated understanding of African American activism and associated outcomes. It has also added more complexity to the meanings of African American identity and citizenship in the face of the morphing, hydra-like nature of American racism. A short summary of these two articles is useful to help us sort through the debate and to encourage us think in more complicated ways about the history of African American struggles for equality.

Professor Hall's essay explores key questions and ideas about what scholars refer to as the Long Civil Rights Movement." Dr. Hall challenges the current dominant narrative of the Modern Civil Rights Movement as primarily situated between the 1954 *Brown v. Board of Education* Supreme Court decision, which found segregation in public education unconstitutional, and the passage of the Civil Rights Act of 1964 and Voting Rights Act of 1965. Hall's "long movement" thesis argues that the beginnings are more accurately found in the 1930s and 1940s era of New Deal and World War II contestations. Hall charts the emergence of political conservatism as a countermovement to civil rights

---

1   Jacquelyn Dowd Hall, "The Long Civil Rights Movement and the Political Uses of the Past," *Journal of American History* 90, no. 4 (March 2005): 1233–1263; and Sundiata Keita Cha-Jua and Clarence Lang, "The 'Long Movement' as Vampire: Temporal and Spatial Fallacies in Recent Black Freedom Studies" *The Journal of African American History* 92, no. 2 (Spring 2007): 265–288.

initiatives that proved pivotal in undermining efforts to secure racial equality. The roots of this conservative political agenda are found in anticommunism witch-hunts of the World War II era that fractured liberal coalitions of activists that championed race and class solidarity by associating civil rights with communism.

Professors Cha-Jua and Long critique the Long Civil Rights Movement thesis on several fronts. First, they argue that much of the new "Long Movement" scholarship stretches and relocates the beginnings and endings of the Civil Rights Movement "past the point of their explanatory power . . . [treating] Civil Rights and/or Black Power as virtually eternal, like a vampire." Simply put, the movement must begin and end somewhere, or the discourse becomes decidedly ahistorical and fruitless. Second, they question collapsing major movements for racial equality—namely Civil Rights and Black Power—into one large, long, shared movement, because this denies the uniqueness in ideologies and strategies engineered across protest communities. Third, the "Black Liberation Movement" has had many local upsurges, which encourages the recognition of regional distinctions. In an effort to welcome similar historical sophistication, this volume will use the phrase "Black Liberation Movement(s)" to encapsulate the rich diversity of movement strategies, ideologies, and upsurges since the abolition of slavery and the Reconstruction Era, paying particular attention to how these movements combatted Jim Crow segregation and its outgrowths across the nation.

The history of Jim Crow segregation is complex, and thus the history of battling Jim Crow is equally as complex. Debates about these histories allow scholars to examine important though complicated details. For example, the South was markedly terror-filled and shaped by Jim Crow laws that secured racial segregation at the state level. But the North, while perhaps not as replete with racial violence, included expressions of racial terror through policing and was also shaped by legal segregation. Northern segregation was codified with racist intent and not merely due to class-based decisions to expand White economic options and mobility, which is often cited as the cause of segregation across urban and suburban landscapes of the North. More precisely, segregation in the North was not merely incidental and was indeed purposeful and anchored with law. In fact, as African Americans migrated in remarkable numbers to cities in the northeast, Midwest, and West to flee Jim Crow, racist policies followed them across the country. Thus, scholars are charged to continue exploring the distinctiveness of various regions and movements to battle Jim Crow in cities and locales beyond the South.

Further, if we argue that a breakthrough in civil rights occurred in the 1960s, during which the Modern Civil Rights Movement dealt a severe blow to Jim Crow, we must explain the roots (before) and outcomes (after) of this breakthrough. The consistent theme across scholarly debates is that there has been a sustained commitment by African Americans to resist racial discrimination, racial violence, and racial exclusion in their various forms. The hydra-like properties of White supremacy have expressed as both rigid and dynamic, personal and structural, and southern-informed though national in scope. Thus, protest strategies have required much dexterity, creativity, and resilience. Following is a brief history that provides context to help us consider the primary question of this collection: *Was there a breakthrough in civil rights in the 1960s?*

WHAT WAS JIM CROW?

When the Civil War ended in April 1865, roughly 4 million African American southerners had already recognized a Union victory would bring an end to the system of slavery. After all, most knew slavery was the root cause of the conflict, and Black wartime participation was crucial for defeating the Confederacy. Yet, while millions of Black people began to actualize what it meant to be free using their definitions of citizenship, White Americans remained largely in control, and the transition from slavery to freedom became heavily contested terrain through the postwar Reconstruction period and well beyond.

As many historians have documented, Blacks and Whites had differing interpretations of the meanings of freedom.[2] Black men, women and children interpreted their rights of citizenship as broadly as possible. White southerners, however, sought to define a new postslavery social order that construed Black rights as narrowly as possible. Within this context, African Americans began the long road toward establishing basic rights, waging battles for full citizenship that would continue for over a century into America's Second Reconstruction of the 1950s and 1960s, and into the new millennium. Whatever the historical debates regarding civil rights struggles, the abolition of slavery and the era of Reconstruction provide a useful starting point because of the Constitutional revolution that ensued. The abolition of slavery, guarantees for equal protection and due process of laws, and access to voting (for Black men)—changes implemented by the Thirteenth, Fourteenth, and Fifteenth Amendments—ushered in America's first national experiment with racial democracy. Similarly, expectations of the role of the federal government in protecting rights would forever be changed. While it can be argued quite fairly that long-standing "Black Liberation Movement(s)" were birthed in the seventeenth century when Africans began resisting enslavement, Reconstruction marks a watershed moment for the many demands for racial equality of the twentieth century and beyond.

"Jim Crow" became the term used to refer to the system of legal segregation that emerged across the South in response to Black emancipation. The term "White supremacy" is used to embrace more fully all the ways racial inequality was sculpted and preserved—socially, politically, and economically—and is oftentimes used interchangeably with "Jim Crow." Indeed, it was powerful expressions of Black citizenship that emboldened White opposition to racial equality. The brief experiment with racial democracy brought forth during Reconstruction witnessed remarkable advances in Black political engagement, Black economic growth, increases in Black literacy, and, equally threatening to White supremacy, the emergence of self-assured attitudes African Americans could not fully express under slavery.[3] As much as Jim Crow limited life options for Black southerners, the system was fundamentally predicated on rendering all African Americans as social inferiors. Beliefs in the inherent superiority of Whites and thus the inherent inferiority of Blacks was buttressed and informed by pseudo-scientific racism, most notably in the work of Social Darwinists.

---

2   For more on this refer to W. E. B. DuBois, *Black Reconstruction in America: An Essay toward a History of the Part Which Black Folk Played in the Attempt to Reconstruct Democracy in America, 1860–1880* (New York: Atheneum, 1977). And Eric Foner, *Reconstruction: America's Unfinished Revolution, 1863–1877* (New York: Perennial Classics, 2002).

3   Ibid.

Jim Crow was exhaustive in its reach. The system was codified by state laws, sanctioned in the federal courts, and defended with pseudo-scientific research. Despite the Fourteenth Amendment's promises of birthright citizenship, equal protection under the law, and due process, the system of Jim Crow positioned Blacks as second-class citizens. Four key pillars anchored White supremacy across the South, where the overwhelming majority of African Americans resided until the Great Migrations of the World War I and World War II eras.

First, Jim Crow was marked by the system of legal segregation, most often attributed with the infamous *Plessy v. Ferguson* (1896) decision's adoption of the "equal but separate" doctrine. However, southern states began passing laws segregating the races immediately after emancipation, with some states having done so prior to 1865. Segregation was such an emerging threat to African American equality that Congress passed the Civil Rights Act of 1875 to stymie its spread by making segregation punishable by federal law. In the *Civil Rights Cases* (1883), however, the Supreme Court found the Civil Rights Act of 1875 unconstitutional, legitimizing segregation thirteen years prior to *Plessy*. By 1896, Jim Crow was already protected by state and federal courts and deeply ingrained in southern society and customs.

Second, Jim Crow secured the economic suppression of the masses of Black southerners by relegating them to jobs that reinforced White supremacy. Sharecropping and domestic work were two prime examples that made Jim Crow eerily reminiscent of slavery. Oftentimes, entire families were locked into a series of labor contracts that kept them indebted to landowners and held within the region's agricultural industry. Domestic work was largely performed by Black women in the homes of southern Whites. If not engaged in farm and domestic work, most African Americans performed jobs that nonetheless reinforced racial hierarchies. And while the South flirted with industrialization across the region, the small number of Black industrial workers held jobs in Jim Crow departments, where they received much lower pay and experienced much worse working conditions than their White counterparts. Moreover, the South's convict leasing system unjustly trapped tens of thousands of African Americans in state prisons and then leased them to industries where working conditions were in many ways "worse than slavery," as historian David Oshinsky has argued.[4] As African Americans cultivated their own meanings of freedom, the criminal justice apparatus of the southern states was used to force thousands of them back into the region's agricultural industry as unpaid labor for states or as leased labor that benefitted state coffers.

Third, by the 1890s, nearly all African American men had been removed from the electoral process through various tactics to deny them the vote, known as disfranchisement, leaving Black people almost no way of changing or even impacting law and policy governing the system. Gone, but not forgotten, were the political gains of Radical Reconstruction, when southern states elected Black congressmen and state legislators in remarkably high numbers. The Fifteenth Amendment, ratified in 1870, opened the ballot box to African American men who responded with dramatic displays of political engagement. This political insurgency became a prominent target for White southerners who countered

---

4   David M. Oshinsky, *Worse Than Slavery: Parchman Farm and the Ordeal of Jim Crow Justice* (New York: Free Press, 1996) and Douglas A. Blackmon, *Slavery by Another Name: The Re-enslavement of Black People in America from the Civil War to World War II* (New York: Doubleday, 2008).

with violence aimed at Black politicians, White allies, and ultimately any Black person attempting to cast a vote. White southerners used voter fraud, appealed to racial fears, and waged racial violence to thwart Black political agency and progress from the 1860s to the 1890s. By the turn of the century, White southerners had functionally crushed nearly all expressions of Black political access and power.

Fourth, racial violence was not merely used to maintain political control; it became the extralegal instrument to order society. Whites' use of racially motivated violence served multiple purposes. Lynching and other practices reinforced attitudes of White superiority as mobs publicly destroyed Black bodies to inject immobilizing fear into African Americans who might resist White supremacy. Lynchings also served, as editor and activist Ida B. Wells-Barnett instructed, to maintain economic supremacy over Blacks, particularly those who challenged racial norms by achieving economic independence. In most cases, Black people were targets. In many cases, entire Black towns and communities were destroyed, as evidenced by the Tulsa Massacre of 1921, which destroyed "Black Wall Street." Whites committed murder, rape, and mayhem with impunity, oftentimes but not always through vigilante groups such as the Ku Klux Klan. In many lynchings, law enforcement was complicit in the extrajudicial killings of Black people.

From 1865 to the full-scale establishment of Jim Crow in 1896, African Americans used a number of strategies to resist and alter the system. Throughout the last decades of the nineteenth century, African Americans used legal challenges to fight Jim Crow, they petitioned Congress for continued support for their political rights, they pushed for expanded educational opportunities, they fought against racial violence, they made claims about the importance of Africa to their self-identity, they developed coalitions with Whites, they demanded opportunities in burgeoning industrial workplaces, they created and maintained all-Black socioeconomic, cultural, and political institutions, and they began to flee the South in search of better options in the North and West—only to discover that Jim Crow had found its way outside the South. Historians of the Black Liberation Movements have effectively charted these resistance strategies and have added to the historical record the myriad every day, less obvious, and harder-to-decipher acts of resistance.

MIGRATION AND URBANIZATION

While the most virulent expressions of Jim Crow were distinctly southern in their application, the system found its way to other regions of the country as African Americans migrated out of the South in record numbers from the 1910s through the 1960s. Throughout the Midwest, a substantial number of "sundown towns" emerged as Black southerners began finding their way North. These communities expressly demanded that Black people leave before sundown or face dire consequences.[5] As urban spaces received large numbers of African Americans fleeing southern terror and oppression, northern versions of White supremacy steadily infiltrated the region's industries, rural communities, urban residential spaces, and political landscapes. Indeed, the 1920s witnessed a resurgence of the Ku Klux Klan across the North's rural and urban environs.

---

5   James W. Loewen, *Sundown Towns: A Hidden Dimension of American Racism* (New York: New Press, 2005).

It is fair to assume a scholarly consensus that much of what dominated long-standing Black activism was intended to eradicate Jim Crow and its various tentacles. Whether aimed at securing fair employment, voting privileges, better schools, an end to lynching, fair housing, or basic human dignity, Black activism targeted the assorted extensions of White supremacy. Yet, quite possibly, the most magnificent statement in opposition to Jim Crow was the Great Migration of Black southerners to cities in the North, and a significant movement to southern cities and urban regions. Black people, in search for some semblance of equality and opportunity, left the rural South in mass numbers over several decades, fully aware that racial domination across the region would not abate anytime soon, if ever. The North appeared rife with opportunities that held promises of full citizenship, or at least better options than those available in the South. But as the millions moved from southern agricultural workers to northern urban industrial workers, new and old versions of Jim Crow were erected in their new locations. This resistance to Jim Crow further nationalized American racism and laid the foundation for movements for racial equality in the North.[6]

The mass urbanization of Black America received two major injections from the World War I and World War II eras. Industrial jobs from wartime production coupled with fleeing Jim Crow became clear migration incentives. The migrations therefore add a set of regional questions for historians to consider. For example: How did Jim Crow emerge in northern regions? What local movements serve as case studies for movement strategies in the North? Scholars have answered these and other related questions with rich and engaging histories.

The turn of the century witnessed the growth and emergence of leading institutions such as the African Methodist Episcopal (A.M.E.) Church, the Black Women's Club Movement, the National Association for the Advancement of Colored People (NAACP), and the Urban League. As southern migrants filled urban spaces, their demands for fairness in the industrial workplace and inclusion within organized labor began to surge, thanks in large part to the organizing of A. Phillip Randolph. And, significantly, the era also gave birth to Amy and Marcus Garvey's Universal Negro Improvement Association and the New Negro Movement, more commonly known as the Harlem Renaissance. These two movements would leave indelible marks on future protest strategies. The Garvey Movement connected African Americans' racial identity to an African past and present. The New Negro Movement made clear the roles that artists, writers, and intellectuals would continually play in deconstructing systems of White supremacy and providing a window into a future free of racial oppression.

The early twentieth century also witnessed important legal victories that did not end Jim Crow but provided support for cases in future decades. The Supreme Court struck down debt peonage, all-White political primaries that had come to dominate southern politics, and ruled in opposition to mob violence. While Black disfranchisement continued, as did racially motivated mob violence and exploitative labor practices, these cases nonetheless highlight the legal activism of the era.[7] The Scottsboro Case of the 1930s—when nine Black boys

---

6   Thomas J. Sugrue, *Sweet Land of Liberty: The Forgotten Struggle for Civil Rights in the North* (New York: Random House, 2008) and Jeanne Theoharis and Komozi Woodard, eds., *Freedom North: Black Freedom Struggles Outside the South, 1940–1980* (New York: Palgrave Macmillan, 2003).

7   *Bailey v. Alabama*, 219 U.S. 219 (1911); *Nixon v. Herndon*, 273 U.S. 536 (1927) and *Nixon v. Condon*, 286 U.S. 73 (1932); *Moore et al. v. Dempsey*, 261 U.S. 86 (1923).

were falsely accused of raping two White women and were convicted despite one recanting her accusation—became a national and international cause célèbre that brought together civil rights groups and the Communist Party of the United States. Protests and demonstrations to free the Scottsboro Boys laid the groundwork for mobilizing protest communities just one generation before the Modern Civil Rights Movement.

By the 1940s and World War II era activism, the more familiar civil rights histories moved toward center stage. Indeed, World War II era mobilizations were pivotal to successes in the 1960s. The victory in *Shelley v. Kraemer* (1948) paved the way for continued demands for fair housing. The March on Washington Movement (MOWM) of the 1940s nudged demands for fair employment and shaped strategies for job equality into the 1960s. The legal campaign that set precedence for *Brown* earned key victories before and immediately following World War II, alongside victories for teacher pay equalization. Lynchings had decreased substantially for many reasons, including the attention wrought from national and international scrutiny and congressional pressure. Garvey's nationalism and the emerging Nation of Islam, home to a man who would come to be known as Malcolm X, would shape Black radicalism in the ensuing decades. Meanwhile, organizations such as the Congress of Racial Equality (CORE), founded in 1942, injected fresh energy and strategizing into the movement's landscape that would prove crucial to the Modern Civil Rights Movement. By the 1960s, Black Liberation Movements had pushed the federal government to a tipping point. Congress, the Supreme Court, and the president were compelled to respond to demands for racial equality with landmark legislation, court opinions, and executive orders that shaped what has been called America's "Second Reconstruction."

While issues of equality ought to be clear, studies into movements for racial equality show a complex set of approaches and negotiations. Scholars have adeptly highlighted and debated the diverse ideologies and beliefs about African American citizenship and the most effective ways to claim those rights and privileges. Local histories have emerged as especially valuable in highlighting the distinct features of local movements and thus local realities, which may or may not have been directly or even loosely connected to a national platform or national leadership. The Modern Civil Rights Movement is therefore widely considered a "movement of local movements." This symphony of struggle was as wide (stretching across the nation, with many expressions and articulations) and deep (exploring the centrality of local movements to local conditions) as it has been long.

Yet the Modern Civil rRghts Movement of the 1950s and 1960s and the long of history of Black Liberation Movements have not led to the full-scale uprooting of America's problems with racism. Indeed, the year 2020 served as a gruesome reminder of how little had changed in the United States, while offering some hope as Black Liberation Movements had clearly emerged in new ways, albeit with familiar ideas and tactics.

ENTER MAY 2020 . . .

On May 25, 2020, amid the COVID-19 pandemic, Minneapolis police officer Derek Chauvin slowly killed George Floyd by kneeling on Floyd's back and neck, restricting his airway. Just a few weeks earlier, Louisville, Kentucky, police killed Breonna Taylor in her own home, with the public later learning that the officers completed a virtually empty report of her killing and none were charged in her death. Eight years had passed since the murder of seventeen-year-old Trayvon Martin in Sanford, Florida, by George Zimmerman. Martin, an African American youth, was physically confronted by Zimmerman because of Martin's race. During the scuffle, which was audio recorded by the police dispatcher, Zimmerman shot and killed Martin. Zimmerman was later acquitted on utterly dubious claims of self-defense. During those years, cell phone footage captured police killing after police killing, police beating after police beating. One video after another exposed that African Americans could be abused and killed by police, while most officers suffered no legal recourse or significant penalty for their actions. During that same period, grassroots activists, civil rights lawyers, academic researchers, celebrities, elected officials, news media, K–12 educators, religious organizations, and nonprofit leaders all steadily responded to one fundamental call, that #BlackLivesMatter.

The protests that spread across the nation during the late spring and summer of 2020 were spontaneous in the first few days. In very little time, the organizing that had occurred since the killing of Trayvon Martin bore fruit. What soon followed was a remarkably coordinated set of demands, in city after city, that amplified persistent calls for local government to divest from police forces and invest in services that better serve urban communities. Activists, public health experts, and community voices highlighted that police are often called to address issues for which they are not trained but to which they respond with aggressive force. For example, police are often called to assist people who need mental health experts instead. Policing is also used to address a city's negligent response to homelessness by criminalizing poverty and homeless people.

In response to the demonstrations, local officials gave police authority to spy on protest leaders, forcibly removed largely peaceful demonstrators from public spaces through the use of weapons of war like tear gas. Some cities ramped up policing. Some made changes to police funding and reformed police practices. Yet, some resisted any calls to meet the demands of community voices. Meanwhile, COVID-19 wrought havoc on the United States while other developed nations had mitigated its impact in their borders. Political leadership in the United States failed to develop a coordinated national strategy to handle the pandemic. Instead, states and localities were left to grapple with the virus independently, with some states having better coordinated responses than others. The virus also exposed clear connections between health disparities and racism as Black and Latinx communities suffered disproportionately from infection rates and deaths.

While the upsurge in demonstrations targeted policing and police killings, America also entered a period of reckoning with its racist past. At the heart of the nation's struggles with the pandemic was a highly polarized political house with distinct lines drawn, with ideologies about race fueling the alliances. One broad coalition was made up of a thinly secured kinship of Democrats, but who were primarily anti-Trump in their political leanings. The fragile alliance included voices from a wide array of communities who were distinctly complex in opinions and ideologies. The many included, but was not limited to, African Americans of varied classes, all of whom shared the common fear of random police violence; Latinx communities who experienced policing injustices coupled with the looming threat of Immigration & Customs Enforcement (ICE), with the two often working together; LGBTQ+ people, particularly trans women of color who experienced police and civilian violence because of intersectional bigotry; members of Jewish communities who were the direct targets of the neo-Nazis who anchored Trump's base; a dynamic community of women who vocally resisted the misogyny emanating from Trump and the Republican Party more broadly; and most interestingly, a widely diverse youth ensemble whose generational experience included moment-defining school shootings, a global ecosystem on the decline, and a nation on the verge of what at times appeared to be civil war.

The other coalition represented the lingering endurance of White supremacy, mobilized by Donald Trump and the Republican Party. This coalition included vengeful White supremacist groups, such as the Proud Boys, who received Trump's open approval; Republican congressional members and state officials who demanded that short-term consideration of state and national economies be privileged over human lives as the pandemic raged across the country; and Trump supporters who questioned the science about the virus's true potential and parroted Trump's dismissal of public health experts with language that often equated science with a liberal agenda to control one's freedom. After the President tweeted "LIBERATE MICHIGAN" and other states, some Trump supporters led armed counterdemonstrations at state capitals to protest "safer at home" orders used to slow the virus's spread. Meanwhile, what seemed to be a definitive cementing between Trump's constituents was the steadfast support for law enforcement of all types and the outright rejection of #BlackLivesMatter, along with its claims about the life-limiting outcomes of systemic racism in the United States.

The republic of the United States appeared as fragile as it had in decades. By July 2020, the nation was at least four months into a pandemic that had become so deeply politicized that wearing a face covering—a mask—to potentially prevent the further spread of the virus became, to Trump supporters, a violation of their "rights." COVID-19 deaths soared to well over 100,000, and cities and states where Republican political leadership had mocked pandemic science witnessed explosions in infection rates. Globally, nations began to restrict US travelers to their countries while glaring upon the United States with dismay and disbelief at the turmoil that ensued. By October 2020, the pandemic was clearly beyond control in the United States and had caused over 250,000 deaths by November. President Trump contracted the virus along with several members of his staff and cabinet. Police shootings continued, as did protests. The Federal Bureau of Investigation (FBI) arrested members of a right-wing militia group who plotted to kidnap Michigan's Democratic governor, Gretchen Whitmer, because of the authority she used to contain COVID-19 in her state. As the November presidential election loomed, there was uncertainty whether the republic of the United States would hold.

On Wednesday, January 6, 2021, a mob made up of conspiracy theorists and White nationalists stormed the nation's capital during the certification of the 2020 presidential election, intent on overturning the election of President-Elect Joseph Biden and Vice President Elect Kamala Harris. Some of the rioters apparently intended to hold elected officials hostage or even assassinate them. President Donald Trump and other Republican lawmakers had stoked this insurrection, having spent weeks peddling lies that the election was stolen by Democrats. On Wednesday, January 13, 2021, Donald Trump became the first president in American history to be impeached twice.

With this brief history as a foundation, we can better consider the question that guides this book: *Was there a breakthrough in civil rights in the 1960s?*

TIMELINE

1865	Thirteenth Amendment passed on January 31, ratified on December 6.
	Congress establishes Freedmen's Bureau.
	Civil War ends, April 9, 1965.
	Assassination of President Lincoln, April 15.
	Southern states enact Black Codes.
	Ku Klux Klan created in Tennessee.
1866	Civil Rights Act passed despite President Johnson's veto.
1867	Congress passes a series of Reconstruction Acts to reconnect the nation.
	Republican party platform includes equality for African Americans.
1868	Fourteenth Amendment ratified.
	Oscar J. Dunn elected lieutenant governor of Louisiana.
	Francis L. Cardozo elected Secretary of State in South Carolina.
	P. B. S. Pinchback becomes first African American governor (Louisiana) in the United States.
1870	Fifteenth Amendment ratified.
	Hiram Revels becomes first African American elected to US Senate.
	Jasper J. Wright becomes the first African American to serve on a state Supreme Court (South Carolina).
	Department of Justice created to prosecute domestic terrorist groups.
1871	Forty-second Congress includes five Black members in the House of Representatives.
	Congress passes the Ku Klux Klan Act(s) in response to racial terror across the South.
1874	Blanche K. Bruce elected to US Senate (Mississippi).
	Robert Smalls, hero of the Civil War, elected to Congress as representative of South Carolina.
1875	Civil Rights Act of 1875 provides African Americans with the right to equal treatment in public places and transportation.
	Blanche K. Bruce becomes the first African American Senator to serve a complete six-year term.
1876	In *U.S. v. Reese* the Supreme Court upholds poll taxes, literacy tests, and grandfather clauses.
	In *U.S. v. Cruikshank* the Supreme Court rules Fourteenth Amendment protections only applied to actions of state governments not individuals.
1877	Rutherford B. Hayes, inaugurated President due to the Tilden-Hayes Compromise, returns control of the South to Democrats and withdraws federal troops.
1877–1879	Federal government withdraws troops from the South signaling the formal end of Reconstruction.

The Black Exodus begins as tens of thousands of African Americans migrate westward.

1881   Booker T. Washington founds the Tuskegee Normal and Industrial Institute in Alabama.

1883   In *The Civil Rights Cases*, the Supreme Court rules the Civil Rights Act of 1875 unconstitutional, opening the door to Jim Crow segregation.

1892   Ida B. Wells-Barnett publishes *Southern Horrors: Lynch Law in all Its Phases* exposing lynching and white mob violence as tools to destroy Black economic progress.

1895   Ida B. Wells-Barnett publishes *The Red Record*, expanding her previous research into lynchings and white mob violence since 1865.

1896   In *Plessy v. Ferguson* the Supreme Court affirms the "separate but equal doctrine."

National Association of Colored Women is formed. Founders include Mary Church Terrell, Josephine St. Pierre Ruffin, Ida B. Wells-Barnett, and Frances E. W. Harper.

1905   *The Chicago Defender* founded by Robert Abbott.

W. E. B. DuBois founds the Niagara movement, a forerunner to the NAACP.

1906   Seven students at Cornell University form Alpha Phi Alpha Fraternity, the first college fraternity for Black men.

September 22-24, during the Atlanta Massacre white mobs kill at least 25 African Americans. Events reported through news media around the world.

1908   Alpha Kappa Alpha, the first Black sorority, is founded on the campus of Howard University.

1909   The National Association for the Advancement of Colored People (NAACP) is founded in New York.

1913   The Woodrow Wilson administration initiates the racial segregation of workplaces, restrooms, and lunchrooms in all federal offices across the nation.

1914   Marcus Garvey establishes the Universal Negro Improvement Association, "to promote the spirit of race pride" and create a sense of worldwide unity among Black people.

1915   The Great Migration(s) of African Americans from the South is underway.

In *Guinn v. US* the Supreme Court finds grandfather clauses unconstitutional.

1917   The United States enters World War I and some 370,000 African Americans will join the armed forces.

July 3, During the East St. Louis Massacre, white mobs kill over forty Black people and drive 6,000 from their homes.

July 28, 10,000 African Americans march in NYC to protest lynchings and race riots. Considered the first major civil rights demonstration in the twentieth century.

In *Buchanan v. Warley*, the Supreme Court strikes down a Kentucky city ordinance prohibiting the sale of real estate to African Americans.

1919   Twenty-five race riots take place throughout the nation prompting the label "Red Summer."

A resurgent KKK is operating in twenty-seven states.

Eighty-three African Americans are lynched during the year, among them a number of returning soldiers still in uniform.

Claude McKay publishes "If We Must Die," considered one of the first major examples of Harlem Renaissance/New Negro movement writing.

1920s   The Harlem Renaissance/New Negro Movement flourishes as a literary, artistic, political, and intellectual movement challenging Jim Crow era notions about Black cultural identity and intellect.

1920   August 26, the Nineteenth Amendment to the Constitution grants women the right to vote. African American women are denied the franchise in most southern states.

Marcus Garvey leads the first international convention of the Universal Negro Improvement Association.

1921   *Shuffle Along* by Noble Sissle and Eubie Blake opens on Broadway on May 23. This is considered the first major theatrical production of the Harlem Renaissance.

May 31–June 1, during the Tulsa Race Riot white mobs kill at least sixty Black people, maybe hundreds, and destroys Black Wall Street.

1922   In September, William Leo Hansberry of Howard University teaches the first course in African history and civilization at an American university.

1923   January 4, the small, predominately Black town of Rosewood, Florida, is destroyed by a mob of white residents from nearby communities.

Bessie Smith signs with Columbia Records to produce race records. Her recording, "Down-Hearted Blues," becomes the first million-selling record by an African American artist.

1925   Philip Randolph founds the Brotherhood of Sleeping Car Porters, the first Black labor union.

1930	Wallace Fard Muhammad founds the Nation of Islam, a black nationalist and separatist movement. Four years later Elijah Muhammad assumes control of the NOI.
1931	Walter White is named NAACP executive secretary. The NAACP mounts a new strategy primarily using lawsuits to end racial discrimination.
	Nine Black youths, named the Scottsboro Boys, are indicted on charges of rape though evidence showed they were innocent. This case becomes an international cause.
1939	Billie Holiday records "Strange Fruit," further igniting protests against lynchings.
1941	March on Washington Movement emerges to demand African American access to war-time industry.
	President Roosevelt signs Executive Order 8802, which prohibits racial discrimination in the nation's defense industries.
1942	The Congress of Racial Equality (CORE) is founded in Chicago inspired by Mahatma Gandhi's philosophies of non-violence.
1947	Jackie Robinson breaks Major League Baseball's color barrier when he is signed to the Brooklyn Dodgers by Branch Rickey.
1948	President Harry S. Truman signs Executive Order 9981, intended to desegregate the nation's military.
1950	In *McLaurin v. Oklahoma State Regents*, the Supreme Court rules that a public institution of higher learning could not treat students differently solely based on their race.
	In *Sweatt v. Painter*, the Supreme Court rules that separate education must include quantifiable and substantive equality, in facilities and education experience.
1952	Malcolm X becomes a minister of the Nation of Islam.
1954	The Supreme Court strikes down segregation in public schools in *Brown v. Board of Education*.
1955	Emmett Till is brutally murdered for allegedly whistling at a white woman in Mississippi. The public outrage generated helps spur the civil rights movement.
	Rosa Parks refuses to give up her seat at the front of the "colored section" of a bus to a white passenger (December 1). In response to her arrest, Montgomery's Black community launch a successful year-long bus boycott.
1956	December 21, Montgomery's buses are desegregated.

1957   The Southern Christian Leadership Conference (SCLC), a regional civil rights organization, is established.

The "Little Rock Nine" are blocked from entering Central High School on the orders of Governor Orval Faubus. The Arkansas National Guard is federalized to intervene on their behalf.

1960   Four Black students in Greensboro, North Carolina, begin a sit-in at a segregated Woolworth's lunch counter. The event triggers many similar nonviolent protests throughout the South, led by college and high school students.

The Student Nonviolent Coordinating Committee (SNCC) is founded at Shaw University in Raleigh, North Carolina.

1961   Members of the Congress of Racial Equality (CORE) and SNCC initiate the Freedom Rides challenging segregated interstate buses. The group of Black and white activists are attacked by angry white mobs along the journey.

1962   James Meredith becomes the first Black student to enroll at the University of Mississippi. President Kennedy sends 5,000 federal troops after white rioting erupts.

1963   Martin Luther King, Jr. is arrested and jailed during anti-segregation protests in Birmingham and writes his "Letter from Birmingham Jail," which advocated nonviolent civil disobedience.

The March on Washington for Jobs and Freedom is attended by roughly 250,000 people. The march builds momentum for passage of the Civil Rights Act of 1964.

Vivian Malone and James Hood register for classes at the University of Alabama, despite Governor George Wallace physically blocking their way.

September 15, four young Black girls attending Sunday school are killed when a bomb explodes at the Sixteenth Street Baptist Church in Birmingham, Alabama.

1964   Congress passes the 1964 Civil Rights Act, which statutorily ends segregation.

A collection of civil rights organizations initiates Freedom Summer in Mississippi with the intent to register large number of African Americans to vote.

The slain bodies of three civil-rights workers—Andrew Goodman, James Earl Chaney, and Michael Schwerner—are found, murdered by the KKK in Philadelphia, Mississippi.

Martin Luther King receives the Nobel Peace Prize.

1965   Malcolm X, Black nationalist and founder of the Organization of Afro-American Unity, is assassinated.

March 7, State troopers violently attack peaceful demonstrators as they attempt to cross the Edmund Pettus Bridge in Selma, Alabama. The "Bloody

Sunday" march is widely considered a key catalyst for the passage of the Voting Rights Act of 1965.

Congress passes the Voting Rights Act.

August 11-16, During six days of rioting in Watts, a Black section of Los Angeles, thirty-five people are killed and 883 injured

1966   The Black Panther Party for Self-Defense is founded by Huey Newton and Bobby Seale in Oakland, California.

1967   Stokely Carmichael, a leader of the Student Nonviolent Coordinating Committee (SNCC), coins the phrase "Black Power."

Major riots take place in Newark and Detroit, marking the "long, hot summer" when 150+ riots erupt due to police abuse and poverty.

President Johnson appoints Thurgood Marshall to the Supreme Court, becoming the first Black Supreme Court Justice.

The Supreme Court rules in *Loving v. Virginia* that prohibiting interracial marriage is unconstitutional.

1968   Martin Luther King, Jr., is assassinated in Memphis, Tennessee, igniting a wave of social unrest across the United States.

President Johnson signs the Civil Rights Act of 1968, prohibiting discrimination in the sale, rental, and financing of housing.

Shirley Chisholm becomes the first African American woman US Representative.

1971   George Jackson is murdered in San Quentin State Prison after the publication of his revolutionary treatise, *The Soledad Brother*, sparking rebellions by inmates.

September 9-13, Prisoners at Attica Correctional Facility rebel against abusive guards and deplorable conditions. State police regain control after killing thirty-three prisoners and ten correctional officers.

1972   Rep. Shirley Chisolm becomes the first African American candidate for president and the first woman to run for president as a Democrat.

Dr. Angela Davis is acquitted of all charges after being held in jail for over a year. Davis's acquittal is viewed as a key victory against government repression.

National Black Political Convention (Gary Convention) held in Gary, IN

1974   Founded in the Bronx, New York, hip hop music and culture begin to gain popularity.

1976   President Jimmy Carter is elected with significant support from African American voters, emphasizing the impact of the Voting Rights Act of 1965.

1978   In *Regents of the University of California v. Bakke*, the Supreme Court strikes down a medical school program that sets seats aside for racial minorities.

1986	The Reagan Administration advances the War on Drugs with the passage of the Anti-Drug Abuse Act. Its provisions include mandatory minimums for drug possession.
1991	Rodney King is beaten by several LAPD officers which is captured on a home video recorder. The officers' acquittal sparks the LA riots the following year.
1996	The Violent Crime Control and Law Enforcement Act included billions for prisons and militarization of police, mandatory minimums, and "three-strikes" mandatory life sentences for repeat offenders.
	The Personal Responsibility and Work Opportunity Reconciliation Act limits welfare benefits to five years and requires beneficiaries to secure gainful employment.
2001	Colin Powell becomes the first African American to serve as Secretary of State after a decorated military career.
	Condoleezza Rice, noted political theorist, becomes the first woman to serve as National Security Advisor.
2005	Condoleezza Rice becomes the first African American woman to serve as Secretary of State accentuating her impressive political career.
2008	Barack Obama elected the nation's first African American president.
2012	Trayvon Martin, a seventeen-year-old African American, is stalked and murdered because of his race, sparking national and global responses through digital media.
2013	The Black Lives Matter Movement, popularized through #BlackLivesMatter, emerges in response to the acquittal of Trayvon Martin's murderer.
2014	Eric Garner's murder by police is shared widely across social media, as viewers hear his plea, "I can't breathe," while police choke him to death using a prohibited chokehold.
	Social unrest and demonstrations emerge in Ferguson, Missouri, in response to the police killing of Michael Brown.
2015	The Movement for Black Lives (M4BL) emerges in responses to continued police killings of unarmed Black people.
2016	Donald Trump is elected President despite touting white nationalism and racist imagery directed at immigrants, encouraging violence toward political opponents, and encouraging sexual assault and violence toward women.
2017	White supremacist organizations hold a Unite the Right rally in Charlottesville, Virginia, that leads to the death of Heather Heyer, who was there to protest the rally.
2018	The March for Our Lives converges on Washington, DC to demand legislation to prevent gun violence.

2020   The deaths of Ahmaud Arbery, Breonna Taylor, and George Floyd spark national and international movements against police violence and white supremacy.

The coronavirus pandemic ravages the globe. The United States is especially impacted with African Americans experiencing particular disparities.

Senator Kamala Harris becomes the first African American, Asian American, and woman to be elected vice president. And the highest-ranking woman elected official in US history.

HISTORIANS' CONVERSATIONS

POSITION #1—THE 1960S
BREAKTHROUGH IN CIVIL RIGHTS

During the 1950s and 1960s, African American challenges to Jim Crow ushered in dramatic changes to America's racial and political order. As the Modern Civil Rights Movement concluded, African American activism gave rise to improved employment opportunities, greater access to education, renewed political engagement, and the range of opportunities that emerge from these cornerstones to social mobility. By the 1970s, African Americans garnered the political power to elect Black officials to local, state, and federal offices—a development that had not occurred in comparable scale since the Reconstruction Era. Indeed, a breakthrough in civil rights and racial equality had occurred.

But challenges to American racism were not new. In the hundred years since emancipation, African Americans had leveled ongoing protests and challenges to Jim Crow. However, by the 1960s the system of racial segregation had reached a tipping point due to a level of coordination across protest strategies and protest communities unlike ever before. It was this coordination of protest, a symphony of struggle, that ultimately led to the historic victories and outcomes of the 1960s, bearing fruit into the 1970s. Legal activism, lobbying Congress, nonviolent direct action, literary and artistic commentary, radical nationalism, international solidarity, and the wide-scale synergy between the Black working class and middle class at the local level provided the Modern Civil Rights Movement a level of coordination not engendered in previous eras. Organizations merged, creating new coalitions from existing alliances; strategies and tactics were redirected and reimagined; meanwhile some groups stayed on courses previously charted. Indeed, it was this coordination across the many activists and organizations, which also promoted success in key civil rights arenas, that ultimately toppled the edifice of Jim Crow.

Because Jim Crow was anchored and propelled by law, legal activism challenging the constitutionality of segregation focused on nearly every aspect of the system. Legal victories over segregation ultimately cleared the path toward outlawing Jim Crow by the mid-1960s. Legal challenges targeted racial segregation in public accommodations and conveyances, racial exclusion or other racially motivated practices in public education, racial disfranchisement, racially exclusionary housing, racially motivated mob violence, racial bias in employment, and racial bias in the justice system. The National Association for the Advancement of Colored People (NAACP)—Legal Defense Fund led many of the seminal cases across five decades of coordinated legal challenges (1930s–1970s) and were joined in this crusade by other public interest legal institutions.

Collectively, the various legal campaigns and victories would render Jim Crow and its progeny unconstitutional.

But these legal campaigns were not simply the outgrowth of the ingenuity of crafty lawyers. Local activists from the communities out of which the cases emerged made legal victories possible by first being brave enough to file suit. Local plaintiffs and supporters faced reprisals that included violence, job loss, and other forms of harassment. Local people also helped gather a range of resources to support the cases. And local communities heralded the importance of the cases and ensuing victories because of the significance and impact to their homes, schools, churches, communities, and workplaces.

While *Brown v. Board of Education* (1954) has rightfully earned credit for serving as the launching pad to the Modern Civil Rights Movement of the 1950s and 1960s, it was one of many landmark decisions (both before and after 1954) that collectively redirected the federal courts to recognize the legal fallacy inherent in Jim Crow's separate but equal doctrine, which generally operated as separate and grossly unequal. By the 1970s, the civil rights legal community had convinced the Supreme Court to recognize the importance of looking beyond whether individuals were treated fairly to determine if institutional cultures still carried lingering biases that preserved less obvious forms of discrimination. Once civil rights lawyers showed segregation was inherently unjust, subsequent legal campaigns sought to dismantle structural racism.

As legal challenges swayed the courts to strike down Jim Crow, the NAACP and other policy-minded groups directed energy and attention to gaining voice in a Congress that remained immovable on civil rights due to southern Democrats who openly supported and protected segregation. These segregationists, referred to as "Dixiecrats," were unabashed in their stances, which were articulated in the *Southern Manifesto* in 1956. The *Southern Manifesto* called for the outright defiance and resistance to *Brown*, along with the preservation of segregation in defiance of the Supreme Court's landmark ruling.

Despite oppositions from Dixiecrats, the civil rights community was aggressive in its lobbying efforts. In fact, lobbying efforts in Washington, DC, were central to the passage of the momentous civil rights legislation of the 1960s. Civil rights lobbyists, along with activists who shaped the earth-quaking voting campaigns of the 1960s, helped force changes to the nation's political order. Voting rights campaigns such as 1964's Freedom Summer and those in Selma and Montgomery in 1965 serve as bookends to the era of nonviolent, mass direct action and continue to tug at our nation's heartstrings over fifty years later. Indeed, voting and political power mattered. Immediately after the passage of the Voting Rights Act of 1965, African America voter turnout and the election of Black officials soared to heights not witnessed since Reconstruction. Indeed, Shirley Chisolm's political career, as the first Black woman elected to Congress (1968) and the first African American to run for President of the United States (1972) highlights the speed and impact of Black political re-engagement. This political agency also forced an overhaul in the Democratic Party as the Dixiecrats steadily fled to join the Republican Party, ultimately redirecting the Republican Party to embrace their anti–civil rights agenda.

The impact and power of nonviolent, civil disobedience cannot be overstated. Neither can the role of grassroots organizing be overstated. For over five decades, Ella Baker was the premier grassroots organizer traversing labor, civil rights, gender-based, and youth movement communities. The Modern Civil Rights Movement was further catapulted by the spiritual authority of the movement's clergy leadership as embodied by Dr. Martin Luther King, Jr. The overwhelming impact of the various strategies employed under the umbrella of nonviolence serves as a hallowed example of organized resistance in a democratic society. During the movement years and for generations to come, there have been irrefutable occurrences of American citizens peacefully requesting rights entitled to African Americans by constitutional protections of birthright citizenship enshrined in the Fourteenth Amendment. They were children. They were women. They were veterans. They were clergy. They were nonviolent. Yet, across the country, civil rights activists were met with extreme violence by counter-protestors and often by law enforcement, the very officials whose jobs were to protect them.

The various tactics employed throughout the era were methodically planned, rehearsed, and executed. In some cases, impromptu protest also drew on these more carefully planned protest strategies as models. And while generational divides led to conflicting opinions and rifts between young and old, the synergy born from intergenerational collaborations merged important, though sometimes differing, strategies throughout the era. With historical certainty—freedom riders, sit-inners, marchers, boycotters, organizers—displayed a moral regality forever preserved by the moving image. This revolution was indeed televised.

Few, however, knew how to manipulate their time on screen with the mastery of the young man who became known as, and popularized the term, "the GOAT": the Greatest of All Time, Muhammad Ali, born Cassius Marcellus Clay. Ali was part of an important collective of entertainment figures who joined the cause to battle racism, bringing the fight to sports, movies, and popular music. Ali's joining the Nation of Islam (NOI) and refusing to serve in the military during the Vietnam War directly assailed a government that protest communities came to distrust given its lies to the America people about the United States' escalation in Vietnam, and the eventual exposing of government surveillance efforts under the infamous FBI Counter Intelligence Program (COINTELPRO). Through COINTELPRO, federal authorities with the help of local law enforcement spied on activists, engineered misinformation to discredit them publicly, incited divisions among groups and members, and in some cases orchestrated their assassinations.

Ali's relationship with the noted NOI minister, Malcolm X, emphasized how younger generation had come to embrace more radical critiques of American racism. As the Modern Civil Rights Movement reached dramatic peaks in the 1960s, Malcolm X provided the rhetoric and attitude to inform these critiques. Ali's friendship with Malcolm X, eventual membership in the NOI, and his conscientious objection to the Vietnam War provided an antithesis to civil rights activism on the national stage, by a boisterous, young, Black radical who also happened to be boxing's heavyweight champion. Yet the goal of eradicating racism was a shared value no matter the strategy or philosophy, as Malcolm would articulate in the years just before his assassination.

The NOI, as Malcolm X's story highlights, reached working-class African Americans who may not have had immediate and regular interactions with the Jim Crow South.

Economically declining, post–World War II, urban landscapes were fertile soil for underground economies, and an emerging racialized criminal justice apparatus had already begun to heavily criminalize Black communities. The NOI is revered for its work with some of America's most dispossessed, reflected in Malcolm's journey. But the NOI preached doctrines that many Whites and some Black people found to be its own brand of racial supremacy. The NOI's beliefs about Black Nationalism included racial separation and control over Black communities by Black people. The Nation's racial dogma stated that Whites were "devils" created by a scientist named Yakub. And the NOI's teachings were found to be anti-Semitic. Malcolm left the NOI due to rifts with its leader, Elijah Muhammad, and began shaping his own philosophies and strategies, prior to his assassination in 1965. Malcolm's theoretical exploration of Black Nationalism occurred amid the civil rights victories of the mid-1960s. By the late 1960s, the Black Panther Party for Self-Defense would embrace Malcolm's philosophies of community-based interdependence. It is important to also note that Muhammad Ali and Malcolm X would loom even larger for decades to come. Ali would become a global humanitarian of epic proportions stemming largely from his public stance against the Vietnam War. Meanwhile, Malcolm's brilliant critiques of American racism continue to haunt those who read his speeches and writings today.

Movement activists of varying philosophies were also joined by a rich community of scholars and literary minds. By the late 1960s, Dr. Angela Davis's incisive critiques of American racism and global capitalism became emblematic of the radical voices that rose to the forefront of this era in Black Liberation Movement history. Born in Birmingham, Alabama, Davis witnessed Jim Crow firsthand and knew well the violent threads of White supremacy. Alongside Davis's intellectual critiques, many were inspired by her call for class solidarity in the face of rugged capitalism and her deep commitment to seeking freedom for political prisoners, many of whom were her contemporaries and were jailed or exiled by the American government. Most impactful, arguably, was and has been Dr. Davis's teachings on the prison industrial complex. As the sixties and seventies witnessed a plateau of activism, Davis warned about and continued to highlight the very issues still facing Black communities today with regard to policing and prisons.

Dr. Davis, though, was joined by a far-reaching community of academics and writers who used their research and pens for activism. A roll call of the era's literary giants includes, but is no way limited, to the following: Richard Wright, James Baldwin, Nikki Giovanni, Sonia Sanchez, Amiri Baraka, Lorraine Hansberry, Toni Morrison, Alice Walker, Maya Angelou, and Ralph Ellison. A comparable listing of scholars and intellectuals would include Zora Neal Hurston, W. E. B. Dubois, Frantz Fanon, Rayford Logan, Mary McCleod Bethune Harold Cruse, Lerone Bennet, Jr., E. Franklin Frazier, Pauli Murray, John Hope Franklin, Mary Frances Berry, Derrick Bell, and Judge A. Leon Higginbotham. (Sincere apologies to the wide array of voices that complete these lists but are not accounted for here.)

Notable figures are important for understanding ideologies that shaped movement strategies, but the Modern Civil Rights Movement was a movement of local movements. While leading voices shaped the broader agenda, local activists led demonstrations that responded to the urgency local matters presented. Local movements were orchestrated by working-class and middle-class grassroots activists who were connected through local chapters of national organizations or who when necessary created their own organizations. In many cases, local activists borrowed and shared ideas and strategies with like-minded activists in other regions of the country. Local activists were impacted by the strategies and philosophies of notable national leaders, but the local movements they engineered reflected unique expertise mustered from within their own communities. Local movements responded to local injustices in policing, education, employment, and politics. Local activists were not simply part of the movement; indeed, they made the movement.

Alongside domestic activism, movement activists were keenly aware of how the US struggle for racial equality was connected to other forms of racial and ethnic domination in other parts of the world. More precisely, the prism of human rights allowed movement activists to recognize similarities in the mistreatment of darker skinned people across the globe, from Asia to Africa and to Latin America and the Caribbean. Activists from across the globe connected with one another to critique the various systems of injustice and to share workable protest strategies. Activists learned directly or indirectly from the teachings of Mahatma Gandhi, particularly the power of nonviolent civil disobedience. Some openly championed communism as a socio-economic and political option, given how industrial capitalism had created a global class of poor, exploited laborers under the oppression of a wealthy few. They also recognized how the political and legal mechanisms of their countries had codified racial oppression, and they shared tactics on how to dismantle those systems. Because of these global connections and critiques, the United States would be called to answer the question of how racial fascism could continue to exist in a self-proclaimed democracy, marring the nation's reputation in global politics.

The Modern Civil Rights Movement continues to resonate throughout our nation's historical consciousness and national memory because of the dramatic changes that ensued. Thanks to the moving image, the entire nation saw these changes emerge in real time, and those images are preserved in documentaries, archival databases, and motion picture reenactments. The unrelenting commitment, bravery, and protest ingenuity on the part of African Americans and allies in the struggle to end Jim Crow racism in the North and South of the country redefined race relations and American politics. Subsequent protest communities would continue to borrow directly from the era's logic and tactics.

As beneficiaries, we are now called upon to protect the legacies of the movement against persistent threats to an already fragile representative democracy—one that has been forged while acquiescing to White supremacy. In 2020, amid a global pandemic caused by COVID-19, the United States erupted with demonstrations against police violence that disproportionately led to the extrajudicial killings of African American women and men, and people of color more broadly. The movements of 2020 exposed how little progress has been made toward true racial equality. The next essay considers the opposing viewpoint that, truthfully, there was no breakthrough, and it asks whether racism is a permanent feature in American society.

POSITION #2—THE PERMANENCE OF RACISM: NO BREAKTHROUGH IN RACIAL EQUALITY

The Civil Rights Act of 1964 signaled the formal end of Jim Crow segregation. The law would go on to positively impact the education and employment outcomes of African Americans. Similarly, it is almost impossible to overstate the vast impact of the Voting Rights Act of 1965. However, after an immediate bump in the overall status of African Americans because of civil rights era victories, efforts to roll back these modest gains garnered immediate and significant momentum. Under the umbrella of political conservatism, the Republican Party and their constituents raised challenges to the policies and programs intended to mitigate racial inequities in employment, education, and voting. This conservative agenda had deep roots in the political ideologies of former Jim Crow era Dixiecrats (southern Democrats) who fled to the Republican Party as African American political participation grew and were joined there by suburban sympathizers from outside the South. This emerging "Silent Majority," popularized by Richard Nixon's dubbing of this constituency, pursued a sociopolitical agenda that anchored urban and suburban racial geographies to preserve White access to employment, education, home ownership, and local and state politics. In no uncertain terms, the forces that worked to maintain White supremacy throughout the Jim Crow era found refuge under the banners of political conservativism.

Meanwhile, the Democratic Party, where African Americans found a firm political home post 1965, did little to secure the sustainability of the political victories and gains of the 1960s and 1970s. By the 1980s, barely a decade after the Modern Civil Rights Movement bore its positive outcomes, Democratic leaders began supporting, and by the 1990s championed, policies that would have disastrous repercussions on Black communities across the nation. Most notable were the Clinton administration's policies regarding crime and welfare reform. Both parties had therefore made it clear to African Americans that the nation's Second Reconstruction was over and any lingering political momentum from the Modern Civil Rights Movement would not be marshaled down paths toward racial equality. So, while there has been some improvement in the educational, socioeconomic, and political stature of African Americans since the 1960s, the United States cannot claim any substantive progress toward fully eradicating racism and the myriad expressions of racial inequality. These fundamental realities therefore suggest there has been no real breakthrough in civil rights. By 2020, as exposed in social upheavals to end police brutality and police killings, and the racial disparities exposed by the COVID-19 pandemic, African Americans had amassed ample evidence that racism in the

United States was alive and vibrant and, quite possibly, a permanent fixture in the nation's norms and institutions.

The Voting Rights Act of 1965 had an immediate impact on ending the wide scale disfranchisement of African Americans across the South that anchored Jim Crow. Indeed, some of the Modern Civil Rights Movement's most remarkable demonstrations hinged on the restoration of Black voting rights. Within two years of its passage, across a region notorious for denying Black people access to voting, one-half of all southern African Americans were registered to vote. Even in Mississippi, a state notorious for violently restricting political access, nearly 60% of Black people of voting age had registered by 1967 compared to a mere 7% in 1964. These spikes in African American political participation led to significant increases in Black elected officials nationally, and especially across the South. By 1975, the national total of Black elected officials had tripled. By the mid-1990s that number had increased from 280 in 1965 to slightly over 9,000. Indeed, some commentators have highlighted that the fruits of the Voting Rights Act manifested with the election of the nation's first African American president, Barack Obama.

Yet, as soon as Black elected officials entered political positions in the late sixties due to the reengagement of Black voters, a disproportionate number of them were attacked by the Nixon administration with surveillance and counterintelligence efforts intended to discredit them. These tactics encouraged harassment at the state and local levels, which was amplified through local news media. The Department of Justice under Presidents Ronald Reagan and George H. W. Bush advanced "the selective prosecution of black elected officials and black leaders." Studies suggest that by the 1980s, 50% of the sitting members of the Congressional Black Caucus had been investigated or harassed through these political weapons. Yet not one was convicted. While the harassment of Black elected officials undermined their impact after passage of the Voting Rights Act, it has been but one tool employed to undercut the political power of Black voters. Recent Supreme Court opinions have severely weakened the Voting Rights Act, while racial gerrymandering, felon disfranchisement, and state voter ID laws serve to further weaken the Black electorate.

The trajectory of voting rights mirrors other avenues through which we can measure racial progress, and the lack thereof. African Americans experienced substantive economic gains in the immediate aftermath of the civil rights era victories, due in large part to legal efforts to embolden Title VII, the employment equality provision of the Civil Rights Act of 1964. In fact, because of Title VII litigation, Black industrial workers in the South outpaced their peers in their occupational standings compared to other regions of the country. This was due to the concerted legal efforts to desegregate southern industry. Meanwhile, industrial growth for African Americans remained virtually flat in other regions. Across the nation though, African American laborers demanded inclusion within the ranks of organized labor but continued to face racial hostility from White-dominated union locals. The presence of African Americans in white-collar jobs increased as well, though still remains staggeringly low.

Thus, while some Blacks reached the middle- and upper-class stratums of society, the actual numbers were and remain comparatively small, giving Whites in similar classes the false assumption that most African Americans had also arrived in these levels. In many respects, gains across employment sectors were short lived. Wide-scale deindustrialization in the nation's urban core deeply impacted Black laborers who had only recently gained access to better pay and union benefits. By the 1980s, Reagan administration cuts to public sector positions would have immediate negative impacts on the emerging Black middle class. Public sector employment had been a haven for African Americans overwhelmingly due to government antidiscrimination requirements. Cuts and layoffs ushered by the Reagan administration hit Black people the hardest. Similarly, Reagan appointments to the Equal Employ Opportunities Commission (EEOC) severely weakened the agency specifically called upon to patrol employment arenas to prevent employment discrimination. By the 1980s, Black unemployment was 15%, as high as during the Great Depression, with Black youth unemployment over 45%.

So, while gains in employment and income were experienced, albeit briefly, we must measure them against raging economic disparities in unemployment, overall income levels, the small actual numbers of Black people in white-collar/managerial positions, and the severe attacks on equal employment programs such as affirmative action. Even the number of Black businesses remained small, with many failing within the first twelve months. The mechanisms that weakened African American employment and economic stability and mobility were firmly anchored by the 1980s. Despite claims of preferential treatment, which were used to attack equal opportunity programs in employment, the nation never witnessed any significant or sustained reshaping of employment patterns along racial lines. Indeed, just before the Reagan era onslaught, Black median wealth stood at roughly $25,000 per family, compared to $69,000 for Whites.

Fleeting employment gains mirrored the outcomes of hard-fought victories in school desegregation and access to higher education. Civil rights era legal victories and legislation called for the desegregation of K–12 education and requirements to increase Black student enrollment in higher education. Token K–12 desegregation due to court-ordered busing was tenuous at best as hostility to school desegregation surfaced across the nation. From the mid-1970s to the turn of the new millennium, Supreme Court interpretations steadily chipped away at the legal foundations sculpted from *Brown* and accompanying legislation. By the 1980s and certainly the 1990s, experts could easily show that the nation's system of public education was as segregated as it had been under Jim Crow.

Over the same period, African American enrollment and graduation from colleges and universities had indeed increased, but these increases were not even close to the surges of White college student enrollees and graduates. From the seventies forward, college admissions processes came under legal attack through claims of reverse discrimination. Much like programs to ensure equal employment opportunity, affirmative action programs intended to increase Black enrollment in higher education could not stand up to the shifting legal climate which had turned decidedly conservative.

The nation's history and residue associated with residential segregation effectively maintains racially bifurcated K–12 education across urban and suburban landscapes. Nonetheless, the growth of the Black middle class gave rise to increased homeownership. Here, too, African Americans have historically lagged White Americans, due in large part to generations of redlining and discriminatory lending practices. Lingering discrimination in bank lending, real estate, and insurance continued to negatively impact potential homeowners even after passage of fair housing legislation in the late sixties. Due to the legacies of exclusionary housing practices in urban and suburban communities, gains in Black homeownership never reached its full potential before the economic crises of 2007–2008, which was spurred largely by exploitative lending practices that targeted vulnerable first-time homeowners like African Americans. By 2010, Black homeownership had dipped below levels not witnessed since the Jim Crow era.

While the racial disparities wrought by this conservative political landscape are critical, one glaring arena deserving consideration is the overwhelming persistence of state violence directed at African Americans. State violence can take on many forms, causing the astute observer to expand definitions of violence. State violence is witnessed through urban renewal programs that sought to redevelop blighted urban areas but had the effects of uprooting African Americans from their homes and sometimes destroying entire Black communities. State violence can also express in the various forms of environmental racism highlighted by recent atrocities such as the water crisis in Flint, Michigan, where local and state governments allowed an overwhelmingly Black population to continue drinking lead-contaminated water. State violence was on full display as African Americans were disproportionately impacted by COVID-19 due to generations of healthcare and environmental racism. Indeed, the state violence that persists today is informed by centuries of racialized control and surveillance which has its roots in American slavery.

One clear connection to the legacies of slavery, and a glaring outgrowth and example, is the racial inequality prevalent throughout the nation's criminalization apparatus. This includes but is not limited to racialized policing, officer-involved shootings, the high numbers of Black people incarcerated in prisons and jails, the massive number of Black people held under some form of supervision through parole and probation, the financial exploitations of Black communities to fund municipal structures termed "policing for profit," targeting black youth for incarceration through the school-to-prison pipeline, and emerging efforts to use GPS technology as a reform effort that would essentially turn some Black communities into open-air prisons. Popularized through the political propaganda of "law and order" which gained political momentum in the immediate aftermath of the civil rights era, Black activists, Black people, and their communities have continually been directly linked to prevailing racialized notions of criminality. In this era of mass incarceration, one leading political response to the myriad social issues impacting African Americans such as joblessness, homelessness, and mental health disorders has been to expand the nation's criminalization and incarceration institutions—referred to by scholars as the carceral state.

Whether racial disparities in employment, unemployment, education, or the enormous expansion of the criminalization of African Americans, explanations for these outcomes relied heavily on the long-standing racialized imagery of African Americans as lazy, violent, less intellectually fit, and overall victims of internalized cultural pathology. Scholars have often referred to the attitudes that informed resistance to policies and programs that spurred Black advancement as the culture wars—sets of implied morality-based ideologies that informed the political attack on civil rights era legislation and legal developments. These culture wars have fueled the growth of White nationalism that is eerily reminiscent of Reconstruction era rage aimed at Black advancement.

The grimmest outgrowth of the culture wars has been the rise of naked White supremacy and White nationalism, evidenced in the nation's political climate after the election of President Barack Obama and the ever-rising tide that led to the election of President Donald Trump. The growth of White supremacist organizations, the mainstreaming of White nationalist rhetoric and ideologies, and public demonstrations led by White nationalists are all indications of the nation's failures with racial equality and grim reminders that anti-Black racism is ever present. Indeed, if we are tasked to question whether there has been a breakthrough in civil rights, we are also tasked to question the permanence of American racism. Because history is neither linear nor neat, we must consider any presumed gains toward racial equality while also considering the persistence of racism deep within the hearts and minds of many Americans, and thus its continued presence in the social, political, and economic structures of the United States.

DEBATING THE QUESTION

RECONSTRUCTION AND THE MEANING OF FREEDOM

1.1   RECONSTRUCTION ERA AMENDMENTS

Chattel slavery defined race relations in the United States from its inception and continues to impact racial formations nearly 160 years after its abolition. Indeed, several provisions of the United States Constitution make direct reference to slavery, though the actual word does not appear in the document until the ratification of the Thirteenth Amendment in 1865. Reconstruction ushered in a constitutional revolution that dramatically redefined American citizenship. As a result of the Thirteenth and Fourteenth Amendments, millions of African Americans found constitutional protections for their rights of citizenship. While the nation's First Reconstruction and the nation's first experiment with a racial democracy became contested terrain legally and politically, Black people interpreted their rights of citizenship as broadly as possible. Similarly, the Reconstruction era amendments provide the foundation for legal battles that would become central to the long-standing Black Liberation Movement(s).

GUIDING QUESTIONS:

1. What role(s) has law played in shaping race relations?
2. What do these Amendments and clauses teach us about slavery and citizenship?

AMENDMENT XIII, DECEMBER 6, 1865

1. Neither slavery nor involuntary servitude, except as a punishment for crime whereof the party shall have been duly convicted, shall exist within the United States, or any place subject to their jurisdiction.
2. Congress shall have power to enforce this article by appropriate legislation.

AMENDMENT XIV, JULY 9, 1868

1. All persons born or naturalized in the United States, and subject to the jurisdiction thereof, are citizens of the United States and of the State wherein they reside. No State shall make or enforce any law which shall abridge the privileges or immunities of citizens of the United States; nor shall any State deprive any person of life, liberty, or property, without due process of law; nor deny to any person within its jurisdiction the equal protection of the laws.

2. Representatives shall be apportioned among the several States according to their respective numbers, counting the whole number of persons in each State, excluding Indians not taxed. But when the right to vote at any election for the choice of electors for President and Vice-President of the United States, Representatives in Congress, the Executive and Judicial officers of a State, or the members of the Legislature thereof, is denied to any of the male inhabitants of such State, being twenty-one years of age, and citizens of the United States, or in any way abridged, except for participation in rebellion, or other crime, the basis of representation therein shall be reduced in the proportion which the number of such male citizens shall bear to the whole number of male citizens twenty-one years of age in such State.
3. No person shall be a Senator or Representative in Congress, or elector of President and Vice-President, or hold any office, civil or military, under the United States, or under any State, who,

From the United States Constitution.

having previously taken an oath, as a member of Congress, or as an officer of the United States, or as a member of any State legislature, or as an executive or judicial officer of any State, to support the Constitution of the United States, shall have engaged in insurrection or rebellion against the same, or given aid or comfort to the enemies thereof. But Congress may by a vote of two-thirds of each House, remove such disability. . . .

4. The Congress shall have power to enforce, by appropriate legislation, the provisions of this article.

AMENDMENT XV, FEBRUARY 3, 1870

1. The right of citizens of the United States to vote shall not be denied or abridged by the United States or by any State on account of race, color, or previous condition of servitude.

2. The Congress shall have power to enforce this article by appropriate legislation.

DRAWING CONCLUSIONS:

1. Does the Thirteenth Amendment abolish all forms of slavery? Explain the clause "except as punishment for a crime" and it purposes.

2. Did the eradication of slavery guarantee full citizenship? Why or why not?

3. Why was it necessary for Congress to ratify the Fourteenth Amendment?

4. Does the Fifteenth Amendment confer the right to vote?

1.2 BLACK CODES OF MISSISSIPPI, 1865

Well before the ending of the Civil War and the ratification of the Thirteenth Amendment, African Americans had begun to shape their own definitions and meanings of freedom. White southerners, however, sought to limit and undermine Black freedom and citizenship in order to maintain control over Black labor, to maintain control over southern politics, and to continue White cultural dominance across the region. Southern states therefore reacted to the abolition of slavery by enacting a series of laws designed to maintain this desired control over the lives and labor of African Americans. These laws, known collectively as "Black Codes," varied in specifics from state to state, but the goals were generally the same: to keep Black people enslaved using state laws despite the Thirteenth Amendment. These laws also set into motion infamous practices such as convict leasing, and they are the early harbingers of how law and policy maintain White supremacy despite constitutional protections of equal protection and due process.

GUIDING QUESTIONS:

1. Did slavery end in 1865 with the Thirteenth Amendment? How do the "Black Codes" preserve slavery?
2. The "Black Codes" made southern states the masters of former slaves. Explain why scholars interpret the Black Codes this way?
3. How do the "Black Codes" codify White supremacy after slavery is abolished?

BLACK CODE OF MISSISSIPPI, 1865

1. CIVIL RIGHTS OF FREEDMEN IN MISSISSIPPI

Sec. 1. *Be it enacted,* . . . That all freedmen, free negroes, and mulattoes may sue and be sued . . . and may acquire personal property . . . and may dispose of the same in the same manner and to the same extent that white persons may: *Provided,* That the provisions of this section shall not be so construed as to allow any freedman, free negro, or mulatto to rent or lease any lands or tenements except in incorporated cities or towns, in which places the corporate authorities shall control the same . . .

Sec. 3. . . . All freedmen, free negroes, or mulattoes who do now and have here before lived and cohabited together as husband and wife shall be taken and held in law as legally married, and the issue shall be taken and held as legitimate for all purposes; that

it shall not be lawful for any freedman, free negro, or mulatto to intermarry with any white person; nor for any white person to intermarry with any freedman, free negro, or mulatto; and any person who shall so intermarry, shall be deemed guilty of felony, and on conviction thereof shall be confined in the State penitentiary for life; and those shall be deemed freedmen, free negroes, and mulattoes who are of pure negro blood, and those descended from a negro to the third generation, inclusive, though one ancestor in each generation may have been a white person. . . .

Sec. 6. . . . All contracts for labor made with freedmen, free negroes, and mulattoes for a longer period than one month shall be in writing, and in duplicate, attested and read to said freedman, free negro, or mulatto by a beat, city or county officer, or two disinterested white persons of the county in which the labor is to be performed, of which each party shall

From Henry Steele Commager, *Documents in American History* (1973), Laws of Mississippi, 1865, p. 82.

have one; and said contracts shall be taken and held as entire contracts, and if the laborer shall quit the service of the employer before the expiration of his term of service, without good cause, he shall forfeit his wages for that year up to the time of quitting.

Sec. 7. . . . Every civil officer shall, and every person may, arrest and carry back to his or her legal employer any freedman, free negro, or mulatto who shall have quit the service of his or her employer before the expiration of his or her term of service without good cause; and said officer and person shall he entitled to receive for arresting and carrying back every deserting employee aforesaid the sum of five dollars, and ten cents per mile from the place of arrest to the place of delivery; and the same shall be paid by the employer, and held as a set-off for so much against the wages of said deserting employee...

Sec. 9. . . . If any person shall persuade or attempt to persuade, entice, or cause any freedman, free negro, or mulatto to desert from the legal employment of any person before the expiration of his or her term of service, or shall knowingly employ any such deserting freedman, free negro, or mulatto, or shall knowingly give or sell to any such deserting freedman, free negro, or mulatto, any food, raiment, or other thing, he or she shall be guilty of misdemeanor, and, upon conviction, shall be fined not less than twenty-five dollars and not more than two hundred dollars and the costs; and if said fine and costs shall not be immediately paid, the court shall sentence said convict to not exceeding two months' imprisonment in the county jail and he or she shall moreover be liable to the party injured in damages...

2. MISSISSIPPI APPRENTICE LAW (LAWS OF MISSISSIPPI, 1865, P. 86)

Sec. 1. . . . It shall be the duty of all sheriffs, justices of the peace, and other civil officers of the several counties in this State, to report to the probate courts of their respective counties semi-annually, at the January and July terms of said courts, all freedmen, free negroes, and mulattoes, under the age of eighteen, in their respective counties, beats or districts, who are orphans, or whose parent or parents have not the means or who refuse to provide for and support said minors; and thereupon it shall be the duty of said probate court to

order the clerk of said court to apprentice said minors to some competent and suitable person, on such terms as the court may direct, having a particular care to the interest of said minor . . .

Sec. 3. . . . In the management and control of said apprentice, said master or mistress shall have the power to inflict such moderate corporal chastisement as a father or guardian is allowed to inflict on his or her child or ward at common law. *Provided*, that in no case shall cruel or inhuman punishment inflicted.

Sec. 4. . . . If any apprentice shall leave the employment of his or her master or mistress, without his or her consent, said master or mistress may pursue and recapture said apprentice, and bring him or her before any justice of the peace of the county, whose duty it shall be to remand said apprentice to the service of his or her master or mistress; and in the event of a refusal on the part of said apprentice so to return, then said justice shall commit said apprentice to the jail of said county . . . and if the court shall be of opinion that said apprentice left the employment of his or her master or mistress without good cause, to order him or her to be punished, as provided for the punishment of hired freedmen, as may be from time to time provided for by law for desertion, until he or she shall agree return to the service of his or her master or mistress...if the court shall believe that said apprentice had good cause to quit his said master or mistress, the court shall discharge said apprentice from said indenture, and also enter a judgment against the master or mistress for not more than one hundred dollars, for the use and benefit of said apprentice . . .

3. MISSISSIPPI VAGRANT LAW (LAWS OF MISSISSIPPI, 1865, P. 90)

Sec. 1. *Be it enacted*, etc. . . . That all rogues and vagabonds, idle and dissipated persons, beggars, jugglers, or persons practicing unlawful games or plays, runaways, common drunkards, common night-walkers, pilferers, lewd, wanton, or lascivious persons, in speech or behavior, common railers and brawlers, persons who neglect their calling or employment, misspend what they earn, or do not provide for the support of themselves or their families, or dependents, and all other idle and disorderly persons, including all who neglect all lawful business, habitually misspend their time by frequenting houses of ill-fame, gaming-houses, or tippling shops, shall be deemed and considered vagrants, under the provisions of this act, and upon conviction thereof shall be fined not exceeding one hundred dollars, with all accruing costs, and be imprisoned at the discretion of the court, not exceeding ten days.

Sec. 2. . . . All freedmen, free negroes and mulattoes in this State, over the age of eighteen years, found on the second Monday in January, 1866, or thereafter, with no lawful employment or business, or found unlawfully assembling themselves together, either in the day or night time, and all white persons so assembling themselves with freedmen, free negroes or mulattoes, or usually associating with freedmen, free negroes or mulattoes, on terms of equality, or living in adultery or fornication with a freed woman, free negro or mulatto, shall be deemed vagrants, and on conviction thereof shall be fined in a sum not exceeding, in the case of a freedman, free negro or mulatto, fifty dollars, and a white man two hundred dollars, and imprisoned at the discretion of the court, the free negro not exceeding ten days, and the white man not exceeding six months. . . .

4. PENAL LAWS OF MISSISSIPPI (LAWS OF MISSISSIPPI, 1865, P. 165)

Sec. 1. *Be it enacted*, . . . That no freedman, free negro, or mulatto, not in the military service of the United States government, and not licensed so to do by the board of police of his or her county, shall keep or carry fire-arms of any kind, or any ammunition, dirk or bowie knife, and on conviction thereof in the county court shall be punished by fine, not exceeding ten dollars, and pay the costs of such proceedings, and all such arms or ammunition shall be forfeited to the informer; and it shall be the duty of every civil and military officer to arrest any freedman, free negro, or mulatto found with any such arms or ammunition, and cause him or her to be committed to trial in default of bail.

Sec. 2. . . . Any freedman, free negro, or mulatto committing riots, routs, affrays, trespasses, malicious mischief, cruel treatment to animals, seditious speeches, insulting gestures, language, or acts, or assaults on any person, disturbance of the peace, exercising the function of a minister of the Gospel without a license from some regularly organized church, vending spirituous or intoxicating liquors, or committing any other misdemeanor, the punishment of which is not specifically provided for by law, shall, upon conviction thereof in the county court, be freed not less than ten dollars, and not more than one hundred dollars, and may be imprisoned at the discretion of the court, not exceeding thirty days.

Sec. 3. . . . If any white person shall sell, lend, or give to any freedman, free negro, or mulatto any firearms, dirk or bowie knife, or ammunition, or any spirituous or intoxicating liquors, such person or persons so offending, upon conviction thereof in the county court of his or her county, shall be fined not exceeding fifty dollars, and may be imprisoned, at the discretion of the court, not exceeding thirty days . . .

Sec. 5. . . . If any freedman, free negro, or mulatto, convicted of any of the misdemeanors provided against in this act, shall fail or refuse for the space of five days, after conviction, to pay the fine and costs imposed, such person shall be hired out by the sheriff or other officer, at public outcry, to any white person who will pay said fine and all costs, and take said convict for the shortest time.

DRAWING CONCLUSIONS:

1. Why were these laws passed in 1865?
2. What behaviors are illegal under the "Black Codes?"
3. What do the "Black Codes" teach us about connections between race, policing, and incarceration post slavery?
4. Explain how the Fourteenth Amendment invalidates the Black Codes.
5. How do the "Black Codes" expose the beliefs that would inform Jim Crow era policies?

1.3 ORGANIZATION AND PRINCIPLES OF THE KU KLUX KLAN, 1868

The Ku Klux Klan, founded in Pulaski, Tennessee, in 1866, and other paramilitary organizations surfaced across the South during the latter part of the 1860s. The Klan was made up of former Confederate soldiers with local cells oftentimes structured using the military leadership from war-time regiments. The Klan and similar groups violently opposed Black political participation as well as Republican control and influence in southern politics. With leadership stemming from landowning, professional elites, the Klan led the charge in re-establishing White supremacy in politics, economics, and southern society in general. This first generation of the Klan operated in small localized cells. The second generation of the Klan expanded into northern urban centers in the early decades of the twentieth century.

GUIDING QUESTIONS:

1. Why did the Klan target Black political participation and Republican politicians/politics?
2. How did the Klan initiation interrogations reflect support for the former Confederacy?
3. Who is the Klan protecting? What, therefore, must the Klan protect against?

REVISED AND AMENDED PRESCRIPT OF THE ORDER OF THE * * * APPELLATION

This Organization shall be styled and denominated, the Order of the * * *

CREED

We, the Order of the * * *, reverentially acknowledge the majesty and supremacy of the Divine Being, and recognize the goodness and providence of the same. And we recognize our relation to the United States Government, the supremacy of the Constitution, the Constitutional Laws thereof, and the Union of States thereunder.

CHARACTER AND OBJECTS OF THE ORDER

This is an institution of Chivalry, Humanity, Mercy, and Patriotism; embodying in its genius and its principles all that is chivalric in conduct, noble in sentiment, generous in manhood, and patriotic in purpose; its peculiar objects being

First: To protect the weak, the innocent, and the defenseless, from the indignities, wrongs, and outrages of the lawless, the violent, and the brutal; to relieve the injured and oppressed; to succor the suffering and unfortunate, and especially the widows and orphans of Confederate soldiers.

Second: To protect and defend the Constitution of the United States, and all laws passed in conformity thereto, and to protect the States and the people thereof from all invasion from any source whatever.

Third: To aid and assist in the execution of all constitutional laws, and to protect the people from unlawful seizure, and from trial except by their peers in conformity to the laws of the land.

ARTICLE I—TITLES

Sec. I. The officers of this Order shall consist of a Grand Wizard of the Empire, and his ten Genii; a Grand Dragon of the Realm, and his eight Hydras; a Grand Titan of the Dominion, and his six Furies;

From Walter L. Fleming, *Ku Klux Klan—Its Origin, Growth and Disbandment*, Appendix II (Kindle edition, 1905).

a Grand Giant of the Province, and his four Goblins; a Grand Cyclops of the Den, and his two Night Hawks; a Grand Magi, a Grand Monk, a Grand Scribe, a Grand Exchequer, a Grand Turk, and a Grand Sentinel.

Sec. 2. The body politic of this Order shall be known and designated as "Ghouls."

ARTICLE II—TERRITORY AND ITS DIVISIONS

Sec. I. The territory embraced within the jurisdiction of this Order shall be coterminous with the States of Maryland, Virginia, North Carolina, South Carolina, Georgia, Florida, Alabama, Mississippi, Louisiana, Texas, Arkansas, Missouri, Kentucky, and Tennessee; all combined constituting the Empire.

Sec. 2. The Empire shall be divided into four departments, the first to be styled the Realm, and coterminous with the boundaries the several States; the second to be styled the Dominion and to be coterminous with such counties as the Grand Dragons of the several Realms may assign to the charge of the Grand Titan . . .

PRELIMINARY OBLIGATION

"I —— solemnly swear or affirm that I will never reveal any thing that I may this day (or night) learn concerning the Order of the * * *, and that I will true answer make to such interrogatories as may be put to me touching my competency for admission into the same. So help me God."

INTERROGATORIES TO BE ASKED:

1st. Have you ever been rejected, upon application for membership in the * * *, or have you ever been expelled from the same?

2d. Are you now, or have you ever been, a member of the Radical Republican party, or either of the organizations known as the "Loyal League" and the "Grand Army of the Republic?"

3d. Are you opposed to the principles and policy of the Radical party, and to the Loyal League, and the Grand Army of the Republic, so far as you are informed of the character and purposes of those organizations?

4th. Did you belong to the Federal army during the late war, and fight against the South during the existence of the same?

5th. Are you opposed to negro equality, both social and political?

6th. Are you in favor of a white man's government in this country?

7th. Are you in favor of Constitutional liberty, and a Government of equitable laws instead of a Government of violence and oppression?

8th. Are you in favor of maintaining the Constitutional rights of the South?

9th. Are you in favor of the re-enfranchisement and emancipation of the white men of tile South, and the restitution of the Southern people to all their rights, alike proprietary, civil, and political?

10th. Do you believe in the inalienable right of self-preservation of the people against the exercise of arbitrary and unlicensed power? ...

If the foregoing interrogatories are satisfactorily answered, and the candidate desires to go further (after something of the character and nature of the Order has thus been indicated to him) and to be admitted to the benefits, mysteries, secrets and purposes of the Order, he shall then be required to take the following final oath or obligation.

FINAL OBLIGATION

"I —— of my own free will and accord, and in the presence of Almighty God, do solemnly swear or affirm, that I will never reveal to any one not a member of the Order of the * * *, by any intimation, sign, symbol, word or act, or in any other manner whatever, any of the secrets, signs, grips, pass-words, or mysteries of the Order of the * * *, or that I am a member of the same, or that I know any one who is a member; and that I will abide by the Prescript and Edicts of the Order of the * * * So help me God."

The initiating officer will then proceed to explain to the new members the character and objects of the Order, and introduce him to the mysteries and secrets of the same; and shall read to him this Prescript and the Edicts thereof, or present the same to him for personal perusal.

DRAWING CONCLUSIONS:

1. Why did the Klan create an organization veiled in secrecy and grandiose titles?

2. How did Klan terrorism impact African Americans?

3. How did the racial violence and terrorism perpetrated by the Klan control politics across the South?

1.4 THE CIVIL RIGHTS ACT OF 1875

The Civil Rights Act of 1875 represents the last Congressional effort to protect the civil rights of African Americans for nearly a century. The Act was declared unconstitutional by the Supreme Court in *The Civil Rights Cases* (1883). The Civil Rights Act of 1875, however, highlights that Congressional leadership was keenly aware that segregation was an offense to equality before the law.

GUIDING QUESTIONS:

1. What rights does the Civil Rights Act of 1875 seek to protect?
2. What does the Civil Rights Act of 1875 attempt to outlaw?

Whereas it is essential to just government we recognize the equality of all men before the law, and hold that it is the duty of government in its dealings with the people to mete out equal and exact justice to all, of whatever nativity, race, color, or persuasion, religious or political; and it being the appropriate object of legislation to enact great fundamental principles into law:

Therefore,

Be it enacted,

Sec. 1. That all persons within the jurisdiction of the United States shall be entitled to the full and equal enjoyment of the accommodations, advantages, facilities, and privileges of inns, public conveyances on land or water, theaters, and other places of public amusement; subject only to the conditions and limitations established by law, and applicable alike to citizens of every race and color, regardless of any previous condition of servitude.

Sec. 2. That any person who shall violate the foregoing section by denying to any citizen, except for reasons by law applicable to citizens of every race and color, and regardless of any previous condition of servitude, the full enjoyment of any of the accommodations, advantages, facilities, or privileges in said section enumerated, or by aiding or inciting such denial, shall, for every offence, forfeit and pay the sum of five hundred dollars to the person aggrieved

thereby, to be recovered in an action of debt, with full costs; and shall also, for every such offense, be deemed guilty of a misdemeanor, and, upon conviction thereof, shall be fined not less than five hundred nor more than one thousand dollars, or shall be imprisoned not less than thirty days nor more than one year: Provided, that all persons may elect to sue for the State under their rights at common law and by State statutes; and having so elected to proceed in the one mode or the other, their right to proceed in the other jurisdiction shall be barred. But this proviso shall not apply to criminal proceedings, either under this act or the criminal law of any State: And provided further, That a judgment for the penalty in favor of the party aggrieved, or a judgment upon an indictment, shall be a bar to either prosecution respectively.

Sec. 3. That the district and circuit courts of the United States shall have, exclusively of the courts of the several States, cognizance of all crimes and offenses against, and violations of, the provisions of this act; and actions for the penalty given by the preceding section may be prosecuted in the territorial, district, or circuit courts of the United States wherever the defendant may be found, without regard to the other party; and the district attorneys, marshals, and deputy marshals of the United States, and commissioners appointed by the circuit and territorial

From *US Statutes at Large*, Vol. XVIII, 335.

courts of the United States, with powers of arresting and imprisoning or bailing offenders against the laws of the United States, are hereby specially authorized and required to institute proceedings against every person who shall violate the provisions of this act, and cause him to be arrested and imprisoned or bailed, as the case may be, for trial before such court of the United States, or territorial court, as by law has cognizance of the offense, except in respect of the right of action accruing to the person aggrieved; and such district attorneys shall cause such proceedings to be prosecuted to their termination as in other cases: Provided, that nothing contained in this section shall be construed to deny or defeat any right of civil action accruing to any person, whether by reason of this act or otherwise; and any district attorney who shall willfully fail to institute and prosecute the proceedings herein required, shall, for every such offense, forfeit and pay the sum of five hundred dollars to the person aggrieved thereby, to be recovered by an action of debt, with full costs, and shall, on conviction thereof, be deemed guilty of a misdemeanor, and be fined not less than one thousand nor more than five thousand dollars: And provided further, That a judgment for the penalty in favor of the party aggrieved against any such district attorney, or a judgment upon an indictment against any such district attorney, shall be a bar to either prosecution respectively.

Sec. 4. That no citizen possessing all other qualifications which are or may be prescribed by law shall be disqualified for service as grand or petit juror in any court of the United States, or of any State, on account of race, color, or previous condition of servitude; and any officer or other person charged with any duty in the selection or summoning of jurors who shall exclude or fail to summon any citizen for the cause aforesaid shall, on conviction thereof, be deemed guilty of a misdemeanor, and be fined not more than five thousand dollars.

Sec. 5. All cases arising under the provisions of this act in the courts of the United States shall be reviewable by the Supreme Court of the United States, without regard to the sum in controversy, under the same provisions and regulations as are now provided by law for the review of other causes in said court.

Approved, March 1, 1875

DRAWING CONCLUSIONS:

1. What does the Civil Rights Act of 1875 teach us about Jim Crow segregation?
2. What is familiar or surprising about the language of this law?
3. Should the federal government protect civil rights?
4. What kinds of comparisons can be made between the Black Codes, the Fourteenth Amendment, and the Civil Rights Act of 1875?

JIM CROW AND THE PROBLEM OF RACISM

2.1 *THE CIVIL RIGHTS CASES*, 109 U.S. 3 (1883)

In 1883, *The Civil Rights Cases* ushered in a legal system of segregation and racial subordination. While the infamous *Plessy v. Ferguson* (1896) came to rest in the nation's historical conscious as the harbinger of "equal and separate" facilities thirteen years later, it was the Supreme Court's opinion in *The Civil Rights Cases* that placed race and class degradation squarely upon the shoulders of African Americans barely twenty years after abolition and brought the legal jockeying of Reconstruction to a close. Yet *The Civil Rights Cases* are important for other reasons. The five suits highlight the injustices African Americans faced accessing public accommodations on the heels of Reconstruction. In response to such mistreatment, The *Civil Rights Cases* also highlight the widely held belief by African Americans that the federal courts—and therefore the federal government and not state governments—would protect their rights.

GUIDING QUESTIONS

1. What do the legal actions taken by African Americans suggest about their definitions of full citizenship?
2. What do *The Civil Rights Cases* predict about Jim Crow and racial segregation?
3. What does the opinion in *The Civil Rights Cases* indicate about the role of state laws in the emergence of Jim Crow segregation?

These cases were all founded on the first and second sections of the Act of Congress, known as the Civil Rights Act, passed March 1st, 1875, entitled "An Act to protect all citizens in their civil and legal rights." 18 Stat. 335. Two of the cases, those against Stanley and Nichols, were indictments for denying to persons of color the accommodations and privileges of an inn or hotel; two of them, those against Ryan and Singleton, were, one on information, the other an indictment, for denying to individuals the privileges and accommodations of a theatre, the information against Ryan being for refusing a colored person a seat in the dress circle of Maguire's theatre in San Francisco; and the indictment against Singleton was for denying to another person, whose color was not stated, the full enjoyment of the accommodations of the theatre known as the Grand Opera House in New York ...

OPINION BY: BRADLEY

OPINION: MR. JUSTICE BRADLEY delivered the opinion of the court. After stating the facts in the above language he continued:

It is obvious that the primary and important question in all the cases is the constitutionality of the law: for if the law is unconstitutional none of the prosecutions can stand.

The sections of the law referred to provide as follows:

"SEC. 1. That all persons within the jurisdiction of the United States shall be entitled to the full and equal enjoyment of the accommodations, advantages, facilities, and privileges of inns, public conveyances on land or water, theatres, and other places of public amusement ..."

"SEC. 2. That any person who shall violate the foregoing section by denying to any citizen, except for reasons by law applicable to citizens of every race and color, and regardless of any previous condition

From *The Civil Rights Cases*, 109 U.S. 3 (1883).

of servitude, the full enjoyment of any of the accommodations, advantages, facilities, or privileges in said section enumerated, or by aiding or inciting such denial, shall for every such offence forfeit and pay the sum of five hundred dollars ... be deemed guilty of a misdemeanor, and, upon conviction thereof, shall be fined not less than five hundred nor more than one thousand dollars, or shall be imprisoned not less than thirty days nor more than one year ..."

Are these sections constitutional? The first section, which is the principal one, cannot be fairly understood without attending to the last clause, which qualifies the preceding part.

The essence of the law is, not to declare broadly that all persons shall be entitled to the full and equal enjoyment of the accommodations, advantages, facilities, and privileges of inns, public conveyances, and theatres; but that such enjoyment shall not be subject to any conditions applicable only to citizens of a particular race or color, or who had been in a previous condition of servitude. In other words, it is the purpose of the law to declare that, in the enjoyment of the accommodations and privileges of inns, public conveyances, theatres, and other places of public amusement, no distinction shall be made between citizens of different race or color, or between those who have, and those who have not, been slaves. Its effect is to declare, that in all inns, public conveyances, and places of amusement, colored citizens, whether formerly slaves or not, and citizens of other races, shall have the same accommodations and privileges in all inns, public conveyances, and places of amusement as are enjoyed by white citizens; and vice versa. The second section makes it a penal offence in any person to deny to any citizen of any race or color, regardless of previous servitude, any of the accommodations or privileges mentioned in the first section.

Has Congress constitutional power to make such a law? ...

The first section of the Fourteenth Amendment (which is the one relied on), after declaring who shall be citizens of the United States, and of the several States, is prohibitory in its character, and prohibitory upon the States. It declares that:

"No State shall make or enforce any law which shall abridge the privileges or immunities of citizens of the United States; nor shall any State deprive any person of life, liberty, or property without due process of law; nor deny to any person within its jurisdiction the equal protection of the laws."

14TH AMENDMENT ONLY PROTECTS AGAINST STATE ACTION AND NOT INDIVIDUAL ACTION TO DENY RIGHTS ...

It is State action of a particular character that is prohibited. Individual invasion of individual rights is not the subject-matter of the amendment. It has a deeper and broader scope. It nullifies and makes void all State legislation, and State action of every kind, which impairs the privileges and immunities of citizens of the United States, or which injures them in life, liberty or property without due process of law, or which denies to any of them the equal protection of the laws ... It does not invest Congress with power to legislate upon subjects which are within the domain of State legislation; but to provide modes of relief against State legislation, or State action, of the kind referred to. It does not authorize Congress to create a code of municipal law for the regulation of private rights; but to provide modes of redress against the operation of State laws, and the action of State officers executive or judicial, when these are subversive of the fundamental rights specified in the amendment. Positive rights and privileges are undoubtedly secured by the Fourteenth Amendment ...

And so in the present case, until some State law has been passed, or some State action through its officers or agents has been taken, adverse to the rights of citizens sought to be protected by the Fourteenth Amendment, no legislation of the United States under said amendment, nor any proceeding under such legislation, can be called into activity: for the prohibitions of the amendment are against State laws and acts done under State authority ...

CIVIL RIGHTS ACT OF 1875 TOO BROAD IN SCOPE AND INFRINGES ON POLICE POWERS OF STATES ...

An inspection of the law (Civil Rights Act of 1875) shows that it makes no reference whatever to any supposed or apprehended violation of the Fourteenth

Amendment on the part of the States... . In other words, it steps into the domain of local jurisprudence, and lays down rules for the conduct of individuals in society towards each other, and imposes sanctions for the enforcement of those rules, without referring in any manner to any supposed action of the State or its authorities.

If this legislation is appropriate for enforcing the prohibitions of the amendment, it is difficult to see where it is to stop. The truth is, that the implication of a power to legislate in this manner is based upon the assumption that if the States are forbidden to legislate or act in a particular way on a particular subject, and power is conferred upon Congress to enforce the prohibition, this gives Congress power to legislate generally upon that subject, and not merely power to provide modes of redress against such State legislation or action. The assumption is certainly unsound. It is repugnant to the Tenth Amendment of the Constitution, which declares that powers not delegated to the United States by the Constitution, nor prohibited by it to the States, are reserved to the States respectively or to the people... .

INDIVIDUALS CANNOT DENY RIGHTS. ONLY STATES CAN ...

In this connection it is proper to state that civil rights, such as are guaranteed by the Constitution against State aggression, cannot be impaired by the wrongful acts of individuals... . The wrongful act of an individual ... is simply a private wrong, or a crime of that individual; an invasion of the rights of the injured party... . An individual cannot deprive a man of his right to vote, to hold property, to buy and sell, to sue in the courts, or to be a witness or a juror; he may, by force or fraud, interfere with the enjoyment of the right in a particular case; he may commit an assault against the person, or commit murder, or use ruffian violence at the polls, or slander the good name of a fellow citizen; but, unless protected in these wrongful acts by some shield of State law or State authority, he cannot destroy or injure the right ...

NO VIOLATION OF THE 13TH AMENDMENT

The only question under the present head, therefore, is, whether the refusal to any persons of the accommodations of an inn, or a public conveyance, or a place of public amusement, by an individual, and without any sanction or support from any State law or regulation, does inflict upon such persons any manner of servitude, or form of slavery, as those terms are understood in this country... . After giving to these questions all the consideration which their importance demands, we are forced to the conclusion that such an act of refusal has nothing to do with slavery or involuntary servitude, and that if it is violative of any right of the party, his redress is to be sought under the laws of the State... . It would be running the slavery argument into the ground to make it apply to every act of discrimination which a person may see fit to make as to the guests he will entertain, or as to the people he will take into his coach or cab or car, or admit to his concert or theatre, or deal with in other matters of intercourse or business. Innkeepers and public carriers, by the laws of all the States, so far as we are aware, are bound, to the extent of their facilities, to furnish proper accommodation to all unobjectionable persons who in good faith apply for them.

AFRICAN AMERICANS AS CITIZENS ...

When a man has emerged from slavery, and by the aid of beneficent legislation has shaken off the inseparable concomitants of that state, there must be some stage in the progress of his elevation when he takes the rank of a mere citizen, and ceases to be the special favorite of the laws, and when his rights as a citizen, or a man, are to be protected in the ordinary modes by which other men's rights are protected. There were thousands of free colored people in this country before the abolition of slavery, enjoying all the essential rights of life, liberty and property the same as white citizens; yet no one, at that time, thought that it was any invasion of his personal status as a freeman because he was not admitted to all the privileges enjoyed by white citizens, or because he was subjected to discriminations in the enjoyment of accommodations in inns, public conveyances and places of amusement. Mere discriminations on account of race or color were not regarded as badges of slavery.... .

CIVIL RIGHTS ACT OF 1875 IS UNCONSTITUTIONAL ...

On the whole we are of opinion, that no countenance of authority for the passage of the law in question can be found in either the Thirteenth or Fourteenth Amendment of the Constitution; and no other ground of authority for its passage being suggested, it must necessarily be declared void, at least so far as its operation in the several States is concerned ... the answer to be given will be that the first and second sections of the act of Congress of March 1st, 1875, entitled "An Act to protect all citizens in their civil and legal rights," are unconstitutional and void, and that judgment should be rendered upon the several indictments in those cases accordingly.

DRAWING CONCLUSIONS:

1. What does the Supreme Court state regarding the Fourteenth Amendment, state laws, and segregation?
2. What did the Supreme Court determine regarding the constitutionality of the Civil Rights Act of 1875?
3. What is the lasting impact of the Supreme Court declaring that the actions of private citizens are not governed by federal laws?

2.2 SHARECROPPER IMAGES AND CONTRACT

Sharecropping earmarked the southern agricultural industry that succeeded slavery during the Reconstruction era and was a defining feature of the Jim Crow South. Individual families replaced the plantation labor supply of the antebellum era. These families did not own the land they worked and were subject to the terms of unfair labor contracts as tenants. These images and contract provide a window into African American lives under Jim Crow and the agricultural industry of sharecropping.

GUIDING QUESTIONS:

1. What stories do these images tell about African American sharecroppers in the Jim Crow South?
2. How did limited access to education place sharecroppers at a significant disadvantage in contractual negotiations?

IMAGE 1 A GEORGIA COTTON FIELD

Image 1 Source: Library of Congress
Image 2 Source: Library of Congress

IMAGE 2 SHARECROPPER

SHARECROPPER CONTRACT, 1882

To every one applying to rent land upon shares, the following conditions must be read, and agreed to.

To every 30 or 35 acres, I agree to furnish the team, plow, and farming implements, except cotton planters, and I do not agree to furnish a cart to every cropper. The croppers are to have half of the cotton, com and fodder (and peas and pumpkins and potatoes if any are planted) if the following conditions are compiled with, but-if not-they are to have only two fifths (2/5). Croppers are to have no part or interest in the cotton seed raised from the crop planted and worked by them. No vine crops of any description, that is, no watermelons, muskmelons, … squashes or anything of that kind, except peas and pumpkins, and potatoes, are to be planted in the cotton or corn. All must work under my direction. All plantation work to be done by the croppers. My part of the crop to be housed by them, and the fodder and oats to be hauled and put in the house. All the cotton must be topped about 1st August. If any cropper fails from any cause to save all the fodder from his crop, I am to have enough fodder to make it equal to one half of the whole if the whole amount of fodder had been saved.

For every mule or horse furnished by me there must be 1000 good sized rails … hauled, and the fence repaired as far as they will go, the fence to be tom down and put up from the bottom if I so direct. All croppers to haul rails and work on fence whenever I may order. Rails to be split when I may say. Each cropper to clean out every ditch in his crop, and

where a ditch runs between two croppers, the cleaning out of that ditch is to be divided equally between them. Every ditch bank in the crop must be shrubbed down and cleaned off before the crop is planted and must be cut down every time the land is worked with his hoe and when the crop is "laid by," the ditch banks must be left clean of bushes, weeds, and seeds. The cleaning out of all ditches must be done by the first of October. The rails must be split and the fence repaired before corn is planted.

Each cropper must keep in good repair all bridges in his crop or over ditches that he has to clean out and when a bridge needs repairing that is outside of all their crops, then any one that I call on must repair it.

Fence jams to be done as ditch banks. If any cotton is planted on the land outside of the plantation fence, I am to have three fourths of all the cotton made in those patches, that is to say, no cotton must be planted by croppers in their home patches.

All croppers must clean out stables and fill them with straw, and haul straw in front of stables whenever I direct. All the cotton must be manured, and enough fertilizer must be brought to manure each crop highly, the croppers to pay for one half of all manure bought, the quantity to be purchased for each crop must be left to me.

No-cropper to work off the plantation when there is any work to be done on the land he has rented, or when his work is needed by me or other croppers. Trees to be cut down on Orchard, House field & Evanson fences, leaving such as I may designate.

Road field to be planted from the very edge of the ditch to the fence, and all the land to be planted close up to the ditches and fences. No stock of any kind belonging to croppers to run in the plantation after crops are gathered.

If the fence should be blown down, or if trees should fall on the fence outside of the land planted by any of the croppers, any one or all that I may call upon must put it up and repair it. Every cropper must feed, or have fed, the team he works, Saturday nights, Sundays, and every morning before going to work, beginning to feed his team (morning, noon, and night every day in the week) on the day he rents and feeding it to and including the 31st day of December. If any cropper shall from any cause fail to repair his fence as far as 1000 rails will go, or shall fail to clean out any part of his ditches, or shall fail to leave his ditch banks, any part of them, well shrubbed and clean when his crop is laid by, or shall fail to clean out stables, fill them up and haul straw in front of them whenever he is told, he shall have only two-fifths (2/5) of the cotton, com, fodder, peas and pumpkins made on the land he cultivates.

If any cropper shall fail to feed his team Saturday nights, all day Sunday and all the rest of the week, morning/noon, and night, for every time he so fails he must pay me five cents.

No corn nor cotton stalks must be burned, but must be cut down, cut up and plowed in. Nothing must be burned off the land except when it is impossible to plow it in.

Every cropper must be responsible for all gear and farming implements placed in his hands, and if not returned must be paid for unless it is worn out by use.

Croppers must sow & plow in oats and haul them to the crib, but must have no part of them. Nothing to be sold from their crops, nor fodder nor com to be canied out of the fields until my rent is all paid, and all amounts they owe me and for which I am responsible are paid in full.

I am to gin & pack all the cotton and charge every cropper an eighteenth of his part, the cropper to furnish his part of the bagging, ties, & twine.

The sale of every cropper's part of the cotton to be made by me when and where I choose to sell, and after deducting all they owe me and all sums that I may be responsible for on their accounts, to pay them their half of the net proceeds. Work of every description, particularly the work on fences and ditches, to be done to my satisfaction, and must be done over until I am satisfied that it is done as it should be.

No wood to burn, nor light wood, nor poles, nor timber for boards, nor wood for any purpose whatever must be gotten above the house occupied by Henry Beasley—nor must any trees be cut down nor any wood used for any purpose, except for firewood, without my permission.

DRAWING CONCLUSIONS:

1. How are responsibilities divided between the owner and the planter in this contract?
2. How is cotton differentiated from other crops?
3. What areas of exploitation do you find present in this contract?

2.3 NEGRO RULE CARTOON, 1890S

Political cartoonist Norman Jennet created this image to enflame White racism and encourage Whites to participate in forthcoming elections. This racial propaganda was coupled with terrorizing violence to remove African Americans and their Republican allies from the political process as Jim Crow is anchored in the late nineteenth century. This cartoon was a hallmark of the propaganda used that fomented the Wilmington, North Carolina riot in 1898 where Whites violently removed African Americans from political power.

GUIDING QUESTIONS:

1. How does the distorted caricature of the African American male play into White supremacist rhetoric and ideologies?
2. Why did the cartoonist choose to place White women in peril in the cartoon?
3. What fears are stoked by the labeling of "Negro Rule?"

NORTH CAROLINA—Wake County.

John Hubbard, being duly sworn, deposes and says: That while working the public roads some days ago, he heard several negroes in Mark's Creek Township, Wake County, talking about the Constitutional Amendment, and one of the negroes, a preacher and neighbor of H. H. Knight, bv the name of Offee Price, said they, referring to the white people, may pass the Amendment, but that they would have to fight, and that the right way to do them, the whites, would be to kill them from the cradle up.

Sworn and subscribed before me this the 29th day of June, 1900.

JOHN HUBBARD,

A. J. MIAL, J. P.

IMAGE 3 NEGRO RULE CARTOON, 1890S

DRAWING CONCLUSIONS:

1. Once African Americans were removed from political power and access across the South, what did this ultimately mean for the emergence of Jim Crow?

2. Why is the incubus perched upon a "Fusion Ballot Box?"

Source: From Norman Ethre Jennett, "Negro Rule," *Raleigh News and Observer*, July 4, 1900, *Civil War Era NC*, https://cwnc. omeka.chass.ncsu.edu/items/show/325

2.4   IDA B. WELLS-BARNETT, *A RED RECORD*: TABULATED STATISTICS AND ALLEGED CAUSES OF LYNCHING IN THE UNITED STATES, 1895

Ida B. Wells-Barnett was an investigative journalist, women's rights activist, civil rights activist, and educator. Formerly enslaved, Wells-Barnett became one of the most important voices of the Black Liberation Movements of the late nineteenth and early twentieth centuries. She was a leader in the Black Women's Club Movement and helped found the National Association of Colored Women's Club. She lent a powerful voice to the suffrage movement, critiquing the racism the permeated its leadership. Wells-Barnett was also a cofounder of the National Association for the Advancement of Colored People (NAACP) and collaborated with the likes of Frederick Douglass, W. E. B. DuBois, Marcus Garvey, and Madame C. J. Walker. Wells-Barnett is most known for her stinging critiques of lynching where she exposed that Black economic and political power were the actual reasons Whites lynched African Americans, and not the false claims of rape. This excerpt from her 1895 book, *The Red Record*, highlights her powerful commentary and journalism which appeared in her books and articles in the leading Blacks newspapers of the era.

GUIDING QUESTIONS:

1. How has racial violence worked to maintain White supremacy in the United States?
2. How have racist ideas been used to justify lynchings and other acts of racial violence?
3. How does journalism complement movements for equality?

The student of American sociology will find the year 1894 marked by a pronounced awakening of the public conscience to a system of anarchy and outlawry which had grown during a series of ten years to be so common, that scenes of unusual brutality failed to have any visible effect upon the humane sentiments of the people of our land.

Beginning with the emancipation of the Negro, the inevitable result of unbridled power exercised for two and a half centuries, by the white man over the Negro, began to show itself in acts of conscience-less outlawry. During the slave regime, the Southern white man owned the Negro body and soul. It was to his interest to dwarf the soul and preserve the body. Vested with unlimited power over his slave, to subject him to any and all kinds of physical punishment,

the white man was still restrained from such punishment as tended to injure the slave by abating his physical powers and thereby reducing his financial worth. While slaves were scourged mercilessly, and in countless cases inhumanly treated in other respects, still the white owner rarely permitted his anger to go so far as to take a life, which would entail upon him a loss of several hundred dollars. The slave was rarely killed, he was too valuable; it was easier and quite as effective, for discipline or revenge, to sell him "Down South."

But Emancipation came and the vested interests of the white man in the Negro's body were lost. The white man had no right to scourge the emancipated Negro, still less has he a right to kill him. But the Southern white people had been educated so long in

From Ida B. Wells, *A Red Record: Tabulated Statistics and Alleged Causes of Lynching in the United States* (Chicago, 1895).

that school of practice, in which might makes right, that they disdained to draw strict lines of action in dealing with the Negro. In slave times the Negro was kept subservient and submissive by the frequency and severity of the scourging, but, with freedom, a new system of intimidation came into vogue; the Negro was not only whipped and scourged; he was killed.

Not all nor nearly all of the murders done by white men, during the past thirty years in the South, have come to light, but the statistics as gathered and preserved by white men, and which have not been questioned, show that during these years more than ten thousand Negroes have been killed in cold blood, without the formality of judicial trial and legal execution. And yet, as evidence of the absolute impunity with which the white man dares to kill a Negro, the same record shows that during all these years, and for all these murders only three white men have been tried, convicted, and executed. As no white man has been lynched for the murder of colored people, these three executions are the only instances of the death penalty being visited upon white men for murdering Negroes.

Naturally enough the commission of these crimes began to tell upon the public conscience, and the Southern white man, as a tribute to the nineteenth-century civilization, was in a manner compelled to give excuses for his barbarism. His excuses have adapted themselves to the emergency, and are aptly outlined by that greatest of all Negroes, Frederick Douglass, in an article of recent date, in which he shows that there have been three distinct eras of Southern barbarism, to account for which three distinct excuses have been made.

The first excuse given to the civilized world for the murder of unoffending Negroes was the necessity of the white man to repress and stamp out alleged "race riots." For years immediately succeeding the war there was an appalling slaughter of colored people, and the wires usually conveyed to northern people and the world the intelligence, first, that an insurrection was being planned by Negroes, which, a few hours later, would prove to have been vigorously resisted by white men, and controlled with a resulting loss of several killed and wounded. It was always a remarkable feature in these insurrections and riots that only Negroes were killed during the rioting, and that all the white men escaped unharmed.

From 1865 to 1872, hundreds of colored men and women were mercilessly murdered and the almost invariable reason assigned was that they met their death by being alleged participants in an insurrection or riot. But this story at last wore itself out. No insurrection ever materialized; no Negro rioter was ever apprehended and proven guilty, and no dynamite ever recorded the black man's protest against oppression and wrong. It was too much to ask thoughtful people to believe this transparent story, and the southern white people at last made up their minds that some other excuse must be had.

Then came the second excuse, which had its birth during the turbulent times of reconstruction. By an amendment to the Constitution the Negro was given the right of franchise, and, theoretically at least, his ballot became his invaluable emblem of citizenship. In a government "of the people, for the people, and by the people," the Negro's vote became an important factor in all matters of state and national politics. But this did not last long. The southern white man would not consider that the Negro had any right which a white man was bound to respect, and the idea of a republican form of government in the southern states grew into general contempt. It was maintained that "This is a white man's government," and regardless of numbers the white man should rule. "No Negro domination" became the new legend on the sanguinary banner of the sunny South, and under it rode the Ku Klux Klan, the Regulators, and the lawless mobs, which for any cause chose to murder one man or a dozen as suited their purpose best. It was a long, gory campaign; the blood chills and the heart almost loses faith in Christianity when one thinks of Yazoo, Hamburg, Edgefield, Copiah, and the countless massacres of defenseless Negroes, whose only crime was the attempt to exercise their right to vote.

But it was a bootless strife for colored people. The government which had made the Negro a citizen found itself unable to protect him. It gave him the right to vote, but denied him the protection which should have maintained that right. Scourged from his home; hunted through the swamps; hung by midnight raiders, and openly murdered in the light of day, the Negro clung to his right of franchise with a heroism which would have wrung admiration from the hearts of savages. He believed that in that small white ballot there was a subtle something which stood for manhood as well as citizenship, and thousands of brave black men went to their graves, exemplifying the one by dying for the other.

The white man's victory soon became complete by fraud, violence, intimidation and murder. The franchise vouchsafed to the Negro grew to be a "barren ideality," and regardless of numbers, the colored people found themselves voiceless in the councils of those whose duty it was to rule. With no longer the fear of "Negro Domination" before their eyes, the white man's second excuse became valueless. With the Southern governments all subverted and the Negro actually eliminated from all participation in state and national elections, there could be no longer an excuse for killing Negroes to prevent "Negro Domination."

Brutality still continued; Negroes were whipped, scourged, exiled, shot and hung whenever and wherever it pleased the white man so to treat them, and as the civilized world with increasing persistency held the white people of the South to account for its outlawry, the murderers invented the third excuse— that Negroes had to be killed to avenge their assaults upon women. There could be framed no possible excuse more harmful to the Negro and more unanswerable if true in its sufficiency for the white man.

Humanity abhors the assailant of womanhood, and this charge upon the Negro at once placed him beyond the pale of human sympathy. With such unanimity, earnestness and apparent candor was this charge made and reiterated that the world has accepted the story that the Negro is a monster which the Southern white man has painted him. And today, the Christian world feels, that while lynching is a crime, and lawlessness and anarchy the certain precursors of a nation's fall, it can not by word or deed, extend sympathy or help to a race of outlaws, who might mistake their plea for justice and deem it an excuse for their continued wrongs.

The Negro has suffered much and is willing to suffer more. He recognizes that the wrongs of two centuries can not be righted in a day, and he tries to bear his burden with patience for today and be hopeful for tomorrow. But there comes a time when the veriest worm will turn, and the Negro feels today that after all the work he has done, all the sacrifices he has made, and all the suffering he has endured, if he did not, now, defend his name and manhood from this vile accusation, he would be unworthy even of the contempt of mankind. It is to this charge he now feels he must make answer.

If the Southern people in defense of their lawlessness, would tell the truth and admit that colored men and women are lynched for almost any offense, from murder to a misdemeanor, there would not now be the necessity for this defense. But when they intentionally, maliciously and constantly belie the record and bolster up these falsehoods by the words of legislators, preachers, governors and bishops, then the Negro must give to the world his side of the awful story.

A word as to the charge itself. In considering the third reason assigned by the Southern white people for the butchery of blacks, the question must be asked, what the white man means when he charges the black man with rape. Does he mean the crime which the statutes of the civilized states describe as such? Not by any means. With the Southern white man, any mesalliance existing between a white woman and a colored man is a sufficient foundation for the charge of rape. The Southern white man says that it is impossible for a voluntary alliance to exist between a white woman and a colored man, and therefore, the fact of an alliance is a proof of force. In numerous instances where colored men have been lynched on the charge of rape, it was positively known at the time of lynching, and indisputably proven after the victim's death, that the relationship sustained between the man and woman was voluntary and clandestine, and that in no court of law could even the charge of assault have been successfully maintained.

It was for the assertion of this fact, in the defense of her own race, that the writer hereof became an exile; her property destroyed and her return to her home forbidden under penalty of death for writing the following editorial which was printed in her paper, the *Free Speech*, in Memphis, Tenn., May 21, 1892:

> Eight Negroes lynched since last issue of the *Free Speech* one at Little Rock, Ark., last Saturday morning where the citizens broke (?) into the penitentiary and got their man; three near Anniston, Ala., one near New Orleans; and three at Clarksville, Ga., the last three for killing a white man, and five on the same old racket— the new alarm about raping white women. The same programme of hanging, then shooting bullets into the lifeless bodies was carried out to the letter. Nobody in this section of the country believes the old threadbare lie that Negro men rape white women. If Southern white men are not careful, they will overreach themselves and public sentiment will have a reaction; a conclusion will then be reached which will be very damaging to the moral reputation of their women.

But threats cannot suppress the truth, and while the Negro suffers the soul deformity, resultant from two and a half centuries of slavery, he is no more guilty of this vilest of all vile charges than the white man who would blacken his name.

DRAWING CONCLUSIONS:

1. Alongside lynching, what other acts of racial violence does Wells-Barnett highlight?
2. Why was Wells-Barnett's publishing of *The Red Record* important then? Can this be related to any similar kind of reporting today?
3. What does Wells-Barnett say happened as a result of her investigative journalism?

2.5 SCOTTSBORO BOYS, 1931

This photo shows the Scottsboro Boys, nine young Black men—Charlie Weems, Ozie Powell, Clarence Norris, Andrew and Leroy Wright, Olen Montgomery, Willie Roberson, Haywood Patterson, and Eugene Williams—who were falsely accused of raping two White women on a train near Scottsboro, Alabama, in 1931. Initially convicted, the boy's case was taken up by the legal wing of the American Communist Party, the International Labor Defense (ILD), who helped galvanize public opinion against the racism of the Alabama court while providing legal representation for the Scottsboro Boys. In 1932, the Supreme Court ruled in *Powell v. Alabama* that the defendants had been denied their due process rights and overturned the convictions remanding the cases to the lower court. In 1935, the Supreme Court would overturn another guilty verdict in *Norris v. Alabama*, this time for Alabama's exclusion of Blacks on the jury rolls.

GUIDING QUESTIONS:

1. What beliefs and attitudes informed the Scottsboro Boys' convictions?
2. What does this case inform us about the history of racism and the courts?

IMAGE 4 SCOTTSBORO BOYS

Source: Attorney Samuel Leibowitz with the Scottsboro boys, Courtesy: Morgan County Archives.

DRAWING CONCLUSIONS:

1. What is the approximate age of each of the young men?

2. What does this case suggest about the experiences of African American youth during the Jim Crow era?

3. What do this image and the case teach us about young Black men and the criminal legal system?

2.6   TUSKEGEE SYPHILIS EXPERIMENT, 1932–1972

The "Tuskegee Study of Untreated Syphilis in the Negro Male" sent shockwaves through African American communities when the story broke in 1972. The existence of the study confirmed long-held beliefs that African Americans were the targets of government conspiracies intended to maintain racial injustices. This excerpt from the Center for Disease Control and Prevention provides a brief overview of the experiment, the ensuing legal battle, and the reparations-styled settlement for survivors and their families.

GUIDING QUESTIONS:

1. What were the healthcare options for African Americans in the rural South during the Jim Crow era?
2. How has race and racism impacted health outcomes for African Americans?
3. How might the history of the Tuskegee Syphilis Experiment inform government-based conspiracy theories?

THE STUDY BEGINS

In 1932, the Public Health Service, working with the Tuskegee Institute, began a study to record the natural history of syphilis in hopes of justifying treatment programs for blacks. It was called the "Tuskegee Study of Untreated Syphilis in the Negro Male."

The study initially involved 600 black men—399 with syphilis, 201 who did not have the disease. The study was conducted without the benefit of patients' informed consent. Researchers told the men they were being treated for "bad blood," a local term used to describe several ailments, including syphilis, anemia, and fatigue. In truth, they did not receive the proper treatment needed to cure their illness. In exchange for taking part in the study, the men received free medical exams, free meals, and burial insurance. Although originally projected to last 6 months, the study actually went on for 40 years.

WHAT WENT WRONG?

In July 1972, an Associated Press story about the Tuskegee Study caused a public outcry that led the Assistant Secretary for Health and Scientific Affairs to appoint an Ad Hoc Advisory Panel to review the study. The panel had nine members from the fields of medicine, law, religion, labor, education, health administration, and public affairs.

The panel found that the men had agreed freely to be examined and treated. However, there was no evidence that researchers had informed them of the study or its real purpose. In fact, the men had been misled and had not been given all the facts required to provide informed consent.

The men were never given adequate treatment for their disease. Even when penicillin became the drug of choice for syphilis in 1947, researchers did not offer it to the subjects. The advisory panel found nothing to show that subjects were ever given the choice of quitting the study, even when this new, highly effective treatment became widely used.

THE STUDY ENDS AND REPARATION BEGINS

The advisory panel concluded that the Tuskegee Study was "ethically unjustified"—the knowledge gained was sparse when compared with the risks the study posed for its subjects. In October 1972, the panel

From Center for Disease Control and Prevention, https://www.cdc.gov/tuskegee/timeline.htm

advised stopping the study at once. A month later, the Assistant Secretary for Health and Scientific Affairs announced the end of the Tuskegee Study.

In the summer of 1973, a class-action lawsuit was filed on behalf of the study participants and their families. In 1974, a $10 million out-of-court settlement was reached. As part of the settlement, the U.S. government promised to give lifetime medical benefits and burial services to all living participants. The Tuskegee Health Benefit Program (THBP) was established to provide these services. In 1975, wives, widows and offspring were added to the program. In 1995, the program was expanded to include health as well as medical benefits. The Centers for Disease Control and Prevention was given responsibility for the program, where it remains today in the *National Center for HIV/AIDS, Viral Hepatitis, STD, and TB Prevention*. The last study participant died in January 2004. The last widow receiving THBP benefits died in January 2009. There are 11 offspring currently receiving medical and health benefits.

DRAWING CONCLUSIONS:

1. What are the lasting implications of the "Tuskegee Experiment?"
2. What is "informed consent" to participate in a research study?
3. How does the "Tuskegee Experiment" lend support to calls for reparations for slavery and Jim Crow?

2.7 RESTRICTIVE COVENANTS FROM MILWAUKEE, WISCONSIN

While Jim Crow segregation is assumed to be a distinctly southern practice, throughout the first half of the twentieth century restrictive covenants were used across the nation to keep African Americans from owning or occupying homes in select neighborhoods of cities and emerging suburbs. In Milwaukee, Wisconsin—a city now infamous for its lingering patterns of residential segregation—the following excerpts from neighboring suburban subdivisions highlight that segregation was codified in the North as well. By the 1940s, all except two suburbs in Milwaukee County were using restrictive covenants to deny African Americans access.

GUIDING QUESTIONS:
1. How did the Great Migration(s) impact the emergence of restrictive covenants in northern cities?
2. Was Jim Crow segregation strictly a southern practice?
3. What were "sundown towns" and where were they located?

❚❚ At no time shall the land included in Washington Highlands or any part thereof, or any building thereon be purchased, owned, leased or occupied by any person other than of white race. This prohibition is not intended to include domestic servants while employed by the owner or occupied by and [sic] land included in the tract." (Wauwatosa, 1919)

"None of the buildings erected upon or in this subdivision shall be used to house either for business purposes or residence purpose any colored persons or other outside the Caucasian race, and the conveyance of any lot or lots in violation of the restriction shall ipso facto constitute a forfeiture." (Cudahy, 1927)

"... At no time shall any portion of said Subdivision or any improvements erected thereon, be occupied by, or sold, conveyed, mortgaged, pledged, rented or leased in whole or in part, to any person of Negro or Ethiopian descent, provided, however, this is not intended to include or prevent occupancy by such person as a domestic servant or while actually employed in or about the premises by the owner or occupant thereof." (Shorewood, 1927)

"No lot or building thereon, if any, shall be occupied or conveyed to a colored person." (Whitefish Bay, 1927)

"That all the sections within which the aforementioned lots are located shall be maintained exclusively as a first-class residential section to be owned, used, and occupied only by members of the white race, unless the majority of the owners at any time owning property in said sections otherwise consent in writing. It is not intended hereby, however, to so restrict the occupancy of any part of said premises, or any part thereof, by domestic employees of a different race employed by an owner or occupant of said premises." (Bayside, 1939)

"No part of said premises shall be owned or occupied by any person other than of Caucasian race, provided, however, that this covenant shall not prevent occupancy by domestic servants of a different race or nationality employed by an owner or tenant." (Fox Point, 1939)

"No part of said premises shall be owned or occupied by any person other than of Caucasian race,

From *Racially Restrictive Covenants: The Making of All-White Suburbs in Milwaukee County*, March on Milwaukee Digital Archives, University of Wisconsin-Milwaukee.

provided, however, that this covenant shall not prevent occupancy by domestic servants of a different race or nationality employed by an owner or tenant." (Glendale, 1939)

"No race other than the Caucasian race shall use or occupy any building or any lot in said subdivision, however, this covenant shall not prevent the occupancy of domestic servants of a different race employed by an owner or tenant." (Brown Deer, 1945)

"No Persons other than the white race shall own or occupy any building on said tract, but this covenant shall not prevent occupancy of persons of a race other than the white race who are domestic servants of the owner or occupant of said building." (Glendale, 1958)

"No Persons other than the white race shall own or occupy any building on said tract, but this covenant shall not prevent occupancy of persons of a race other than the white race who are domestic servants of the owner or occupant of said buildings." (Greendale, 1958)

DRAWING CONCLUSIONS:

1. What do restrictive covenants teach us about current patterns of residential segregation in northern cities?
2. What does the history of restrictive covenants teach us about the racial implications of generational wealth?

2.8 ALABAMA VOTER REGISTRATION APPLICATION, C. 1965

This four-page voter application is an example of the obstacles African Americans faced in attempting to register to vote across the South. It was used to intimidate and threaten potential voters. It required answering a range of question under penalty of perjury. And the registrar often had full authority to determine if the application was completed correctly. Additionally, applicants knew that their efforts to register to vote could lead to violence or other negative consequences. This application was just one of many hurdles; once the application was completed both a literary test and poll tax remained.

GUIDING QUESTIONS:

1. How did voter registration measures such as this application keep African Americans disenfranchised?
2. Which questions do you find most surprising?

From The Civil Rights Movement Archives, https://www.crmvet.org/info/lithome.htm

APPLICATION FOR REGISTRATION, QUESTIONNAIRE AND OATHS

PART I

(This is to be filled in by a member of the Board of Registrars or a duly authorized clerk of the board. If applicant is a married woman, she must state given name by which she is known, maiden surname, and married surname, which shall be recorded as her full name.)

Full Name:_____
Last   First   Middle

Date of Birth:_____ Sex_____ Race_____

Residence Address:_____

Mailing Address:_____

Voting Place: Precinct_____ Ward_____ District_____

Length of Residence: In State_____ County_____

    Precinct, ward or district_____

Are you a member of the Armed Forces?_____

Are you the wife of a member of the Armed Forces?_____

Are you a college student?_____ If so, where_____

Have you ever been registered to vote in any other state or in any other county in Alabama?_____ If so, when and in

    what state and county and, if in Alabama, at what place did you vote in such county?_____

    _____

Highest grade, 1 to 12, completed_____ Where_____

Years college completed_____ Where_____

PART II

(To be filled in by the applicant in the presence of the Board of Registrars without assistance.)

    I,_____, do hereby apply to the Board of Registrars of_____   MONTGOMERY

County, State of Alabama, to register as an elector under the Constitution and laws of the State of Alabama and do here-

with submit my answers to the interrogatories propounded to me by the board.

    _____
    (Signature of Applicant)

1. Are you a citizen of the United States?_____

2. Where were you born?_____

3. If you are a naturalized citizen, give number appearing on your naturalization papers and date of issuance_____

    _____

4. Have you ever been married?_____ If so, give the name, residence and place of birth of your husband or wife_____

    _____

    Are you divorced?_____

IMAGE 5A ALABAMA VOTER REGISTRATION APPLICATION, C. 1965 (1)

5. List the places you have lived the past five years, giving town or county and state _____

_____

6. Have you ever been known by any name other than the one appearing on this application? _____ If so, state what name

_____

7. Are you employed? _____ If so, state by whom. (If you are self-employed, state this.) _____

8. Give the address of your present place of employment _____

9. If, in the past five years, you have been employed by an employer other than your present employer, give name of all employers and cities and states in which you worked _____

_____

10. Has your name ever been stricken for any reason from any list of persons registered to vote? _____ If so, where, when, and why? _____

_____

11. Have you previously applied for and been denied registration as a voter? _____ If so, when and where? _____

_____

12. Have you ever served in the Armed Forces? _____ If so, give dates, branch of service, and serial number

_____

13. Have you ever been dishonorably discharged from military service? _____

14. Have you ever been declared legally insane? _____ If so, give details _____

15. Give names and addresses of two persons who know you and can verify the statements made above by you relative to your residence in this state, county and precinct, ward or district _____

_____

16. Have you ever seen a copy of this registration application form before receiving this copy today? _____ If so, when and where? _____

17. Have you ever been convicted of any offense or paid any fine for violation of the law? _____ (Yes or No) If so, give the following information concerning each fine or conviction; charge, in what court tried, fine imposed, sentence, and, if paroled, state when, and if pardoned, state when. (If fine is for traffic violation only, you need write below only the words "traffic violation only.") _____

_____

_____

(Remainder of this form is to be filled out only as directed by an individual member of the Board of Registrars.)

PART III

Part III of this questionnaire shall consist of one of the forms which are Insert Part III as herein below set out. The insert shall be fastened to the questionnaire. The questions set out on the insert shall be answered according to the instructions therein set out. Each applicant shall demonstrate ability to read and write as required by the Constitution of Alabama, as amended, and no person shall be considered to have completed this application, nor shall the name of any applicant be entered upon the list of registered voters of any county until after such inserted Part III of the questionnaire has been satisfactorily completed and signed by the applicant.

IMAGE 5B ALABAMA VOTER REGISTRATION APPLICATION, C. 1965 (2)

DRAWING CONCLUSIONS:

1. This application asks several pointed questions about the applicant's work and social history. What is the significance of these questions?

2. Why was the Voting Rights Act of 1965 so critical for re-engaging Black voters in the political process?

2.9 URBAN RENEWAL, C. 1960

As the Modern Civil Rights Movement reached its apex in the 1960s, the process of urban renewal was well underway in cities across the nation. Urban renewal refers to the process by which blighted areas or slums were redeveloped for business or government repurposing, and for building more expensive housing. African American communities were often targeted for this process, and in their place arose highways, municipal structures, entertainment venues, and sometimes expanding universities. In most cases, members of the Black community under redevelopment were denied access to the construction contracts and jobs associated with the projects. Many African Americans were forced to find housing elsewhere as a result of urban renewal. African Americans lost homes they had earned, their communities were altered and in some cases destroyed, and these communities lost the socioeconomic diversity that once anchored them.

GUIDING QUESTIONS:

1. What does this image suggest about the process of urban renewal?
2. What is eminent domain?

IMAGE 6 URBAN RENEWAL

DRAWING CONCLUSIONS:

1. Why was urban renewal referred to as "urban removal" or "negro removal?"

2. How has urban renewal reshaped American cities?

Source: Courtesy of the Robinson-Spangler Carolina Room, Charlotte Mecklenburg Library.

VOICES OF PROTEST

3.1 PAUL LAURENCE DUNBAR, *WE WEAR THE MASK* (1896)

This classic poem by Paul Laurence Dunbar, published in 1896, captures the complexity of African American identity at the dawn of Jim Crow. Born in Dayton, Ohio, in 1872 to formerly enslaved parents, Dunbar went on to graduate from Howard University. Though he died at the young age of thirty-three, Dunbar achieved national and international acclaim for his writings, becoming one of the most important and influential African American writers.

GUIDING QUESTIONS:

1. What does Dunbar mean by the analogy of wearing the mask?
2. How does this poem reflect the complexities of African American identity at the close of the nineteenth century?

We wear the mask that grins and lies,
It hides our cheeks and shades our eyes,—
This debt we pay to human guile;
With torn and bleeding hearts we smile,
And mouth with myriad subtleties.
Why should the world be over-wise,
In counting all our tears and sighs?
Nay, let them only see us, while
We wear the mask.
We smile, but, O great Christ, our cries
To thee from tortured souls arise.

We sing, but oh the clay is vile
Beneath our feet, and long the mile;
But let the world dream otherwise,
We wear the mask!

DRAWING CONCLUSIONS:

1. In what ways does Dunbar's poem resonate today?
2. What does this poem indicate about the power of the arts to critique race and racism?

From Paul Laurence Dunbar, *Lyrics of Lowly Life* (1896).

3.2 GREAT MIGRATION ARTICLES

CHICAGO DEFENDER, MAY 17, 1919

From the 1910 to the 1960s, millions of African Americans took part in a leaderless move to flee Jim Crow by migrating to northern cities in search of industrial employment opportunities and some semblance of full citizenship. In the early years of the migration, labor conflicts arose as Black southerners moved into low-skilled industrial jobs once dominated by workers from European ethnic communities. Yet African Americans already in the North found the swelling numbers of southern migrants problematic. While African American newspapers were beacons directing southern migrants to northern cities, these same periodicals were also vehicles to communicate intraracial strife between newcomers and long-time urban residents. The following articles highlight these very challenges.

GUIDING QUESTIONS:
1. What conflicts and challenges do these articles expose about migration experiences?
2. How do these articles complicate our understandings of race and class as southern migrants begin to reside in urban spaces?

"WHERE WE ARE LACKING"

This paper does not like to appear in the role of a common scold, yet it would be recreant to its duty if it did not call attention to some acts of flagrant conduct on the part of our people. Among these there is none that stands out so offensively as the practice as corner loafing. It is not an uncommon thing to see a crowd of two or three hundred young and old, idly gaping about the corners, and especially at the transfer points.

So great a nuisance has it become that respectable women and young girls shrink from running that gantlet of foul-spoken, leering loafers. Professional and business men are loud in their complaints against these insects, who block the entrances to their offices and stores, preventing ingress and egress. We have frequently called the attention of the police department to this intolerable nuisance, but for some reason have been unable to obtain any action.

If our aldermen wish to render a great service to the section represented by them, they will take whatever steps that are necessary to remedy a condition that has become an eyesore. They need not be afraid of adverse criticism. They will be supported in this move by all the self-respecting elements in their ward. While paying our respects to corner loafers it would not be out of the way to offer some timely advice in the way of becoming conduct on the part of our people riding on the street cars.

Enter the cars quietly, have your fares ready, and ask for your transfer at the time of paying your fare. This is a rule of the street car company, and the conductor must see to its enforcement, so far as transfers are concerned, or lose his position. Once inside the car, sit quietly and avoid loud talk with your neighbor. Above all things do not attempt a conversation with any one at the opposite end of the car or several seats removed from you. The other passengers are not

From the *Chicago Defender*, May 17, 1919. http://nationalhumanitiescenter.org/pds/maai3/migrations/text6/chicago defender1919.pdf

interested in what you have to say, and the way you say it may give offense.

A little common politeness, a little of the old-time courtesy which prompts one to say "Excuse me" or "I beg your pardon" gives one the stamp of good breeding and always calls for a favorable notice of the person using such civility.

Gentlemanly and unobtrusive conduct on the part of man or woman always excites a favorable impression. And we must not forget those of us living on the avenues and boulevards. Do not sit in the open windows and upon the steps half clad. Do not arrange your toilet in view of the public. These things should be done behind drawn blinds. There is no reason why a Colored neighborhood should be marked by conduct on the part of its residents that belongs to a day that should have long since passed. Such practices may find ready excuse upon the country cross roads of the South, but people living in large cities are intolerable of such things and mark the neighborhoods where these things are observed as plague spots. The pastors of our churches can lend a powerful hand in remedying the evils complained of. Two or three times a week they have large audiences to which they can address themselves. They can render especial service in dispersing the large crowds that congregate around the churches. After the services are ended those in attendance should be told to leave the neighborhood immediately and not loiter about obstructing the sidewalks while indulging in social chit-chat and neighborhood gossip.

SOME "DONT'S"

A fierce agitation is being waged by certain classes of citizens against immigration of Southern people to northern cities. It is charged that they are undesirable and are supplanting white laborers in various branches of work. In seeking a remedy to prevent laborers from the Southland securing employment and making an honest living for themselves and their families, every vile thing possible has been said and unlawful acts committed against the men and women who have come to this and other cities of the North, during the past several months, while the Southern white is coming in droves on the same trains and we hear no kicks from any one.

It is evident that some of the people coming to this city have seriously erred in their conduct in public places, much to the humiliation of all respectable classes of our citizens, and by so doing, on account of their ignorance of laws and customs necessary for the maintenance of health, sobriety and morality among the people in general, have given our enemies ground for complaint. We consider it absolutely necessary that a united effort should be made on the part of all law-abiding citizens to endeavor to warn and teach those who by their acts bring reproach upon the Colored people of this city to strictly observe the laws, city ordinances and customs and so conduct themselves as to reflect credit upon themselves: by so doing it will disarm those who are endeavoring to discredit our Race.

WE CALL ATTENTION TO SOME THINGS WHICH SHOULD BE OBSERVED BY OUR PEOPLE

Don't use vile language in public places.

Don't act discourteously to other people in public places.

Don't allow yourself to be drawn into street brawls.

Don't use liberty as a license to do as you please.

Don't take the part of law breakers, be they men, women or children.

Don't make yourself a public nuisance.

Don't encourage gamblers, disreputable women or men to ply their business any time or place.

Don't congregate in crowds on the streets to the disadvantage of others passing along.

Don't spend your time hanging around saloon doors or poolrooms.

Don't live in insanitary houses, or sleep in rooms without proper ventilation.

Don't violate city ordinances relative to health conditions.

Don't allow children to beg on the streets.

Don't allow boys to steal from or assault peddlers going their rounds during the day.

Don't be a beer can rusher or permit children to do such service.

Don't abuse or violate the confidence of those who give you employment.

Don't leave your job when you have a few dollars in your pocket.

Don't work for less wages than being paid people doing same kind of work.

Don't be made a tool or strike breaker for any corporation or firm.

Don't allow buffet flats or rooms rented with privileges to be conducted in your neighborhood.

Don't allow children under 15 years of age to run the streets after 9 o'clock p. m.

Don't get intoxicated and go out on the street insulting women and children and make a beast of yourself—someone may act likewise with your wife and children.

Don't undermine other people by taking from them their work.

Don't appear on the street with old dust caps, dirty aprons and ragged clothes.

Don't throw garbage in the back yard or alley or keep dirty front yards.

Don't attempt to make an express wagon of street cars.

Don't forget street car conductors are bound by rules of the car company which the law compels them to obey.

Don't oppose police officers in the dis-charge of their duty; you should be the one to assist in keeping the peace.

DRAWING CONCLUSIONS:

1. What class implications are prevalent in the tone of these articles?
2. What labor implications are prevalent in the articles?

3.3 MARCUS GARVEY, "AIMS AND OBJECTS OF MOVEMENT FOR SOLUTION OF NEGRO PROBLEM," 1924

The Garvey Movement, organized under the Universal Negro Improvement Association (UNIA), has been regarded as the largest mass organization-based movement in the history of African American struggles for liberation and equality. Scholars have suggested the UNIA once counted a membership of over 1 million "Garveyites." The Garvey Movement is central to ideologies associated with Black Nationalism embodied in calls for going "Back to Africa," the push for Black political and economic interdependence, and in the creation of Black institutions. Along with its followers in the United States, Garvey's appeal and followers resonated across the Caribbean and Africa.

GUIDING QUESTIONS:

1. Why does Garvey encourage African Americans to look to Africa for uplift?
2. What are the key aims of the Universal Negro Improvement Association?
3. How does this document define Black Nationalism?

… The Universal Negro Improvement Association is an organization among Negroes that is seeking to improve the condition of the race, with the view of establishing a nation in Africa where Negroes will be given the opportunity to develop by themselves, without creating the hatred and animosity that now exist in countries of the white race through Negroes rivaling them for the highest and best positions in government, politics, society and industry. The organization believes in the rights of all men, yellow, white and black …

THE SPIRITUAL BROTHERHOOD OF MAN

The following preamble to the constitution of the organization speaks for itself:

"The Universal Negro Improvement Association and African Communities' League is a social, friendly, humanitarian, charitable, educational, institutional, constructive, and expansive society, and is founded by persons, de-siring to the utmost to work for the general uplift of the Negro peoples of the world. And the members pledge themselves to do all in their power to conserve the rights of their noble race and to respect the rights of all man-kind, believing always in the Brotherhood of Man and the Fatherhood of God. The motto of the organization is: One God!

One Aim! One Destiny! … " The declared objects of the association are:

"To establish a Universal Confraternity among the race; to promote the spirit of pride and love; to reclaim the fallen; to administer to and assist the needy; to assist in civilizing the backward tribes of Africa; to assist in the development of Independent Negro Nations and Communities; to establish a central nation for the race; to establish Commissaries or Agencies in the principal countries and cities of the world for the representation of all Negroes; to promote a conscientious Spiritual worship among the native tribes of Africa; to establish Universities,

Colleges, Academies and Schools for the racial education and culture of the people; to work for better conditions among Negroes everywhere."

SUPPLYING A LONG-FELT WANT

The organization of the Universal Negro Improvement Association has supplied among Negroes a long-felt want. Hitherto the other Negro movements in America, with the exception of the Tuskegee effort of Booker T. Washington, sought to teach the Negro to aspire to social equality with the whites, meaning thereby the right to intermarry and fraternize in every social way. This has been the source of much trouble and still some Negro organizations continue to preach this dangerous "race destroying doctrine" added to a program of political agitation and aggression.

The Universal Negro Improvement Association on the other hand believes in and teaches the pride and purity of race. We believe that the white race should uphold its racial pride and perpetuate itself, and that the black race should do likewise ...

The time is opportune to regulate the relationship between both races. Let the Negro have a country of his own. Help him to return to his original home, Africa, and there give him the opportunity to climb from the lowest to the highest positions in a state of his own. If not, then the nation will have to hearken to the demand of the aggressive, "social equality" organization, known as the National Association for the Advancement of Colored People, of which W. E. B. Du Bois is leader ... but reason dictates that the masses of the white race will never stand by the ascendancy of an opposite minority group to the favored positions in a government, society and industry that exist by the will of the majority, hence the demand of ... colored leaders will only lead, ultimately, to further disturbances in riots, lynching and mob rule. The only logical solution therefore, is to supply the Negro with opportunities and environments of his own, and there point him to the fullness of his ambition.

NEGROES WHO SEEK SOCIAL EQUALITY

The Negro who seeks the White House in America could find ample play for his ambition in Africa. The Negro who seeks the office of Secretary of State in America would have a fair chance of demonstrating his diplomacy in Africa. The Negro who seeks a seat in the Senate or of being governor of a State in America, would be provided with a glorious chance for statesmanship in Africa ...

This plan when properly undertaken and prosecuted will solve the race problem in America in fifty years. Africa affords a wonderful opportunity at the present time for colonization by the Negroes of the Western world. There is Liberia, already established as an independent Negro government. Let white America assist Afro-Americans to go there and help develop the country ...

The Negroes of Africa and America are one in blood. They have sprung from the same common stock. They can work and live together and thus make their own racial contribution to the world. Will deep thinking and liberal white America help? It is a considerate duty ...

HELP THE NEGRO TO RETURN HOME

Surely the time has come for the Negro to look homeward. He has won civilization and Christianity at the price of slavery. The Negro who is thoughtful and serviceable, feels that God intended him to give to his brothers still in darkness, the light of his civilization. The very light element of Negroes do not want to go back to Africa. They believe that in time, through miscegenation, the American race will be of their type. This is a fallacy and in that respect the agitation of the mulatto leader, Dr. W. E. B. Du Bois and the National Association for the Advancement of Colored People is dangerous to both races.

The off-colored people, being children of the Negro race, should combine to re-establish the purity of their own race, rather than seek to perpetuate the abuse of both races. That is to say, all elements of the

Negro race should be encouraged to get together and form themselves into a healthy whole, rather than seeking to lose their identities through miscegenation and social intercourse with the white race. These statements are made because we desire an honest solution of the problem and no flattery or deception will bring that about ...

The Universal Negro Improvement Association is composed of all shades of Negroes – blacks, mulattoes and yellows, who are all working honestly for the purification of their race, and for a sympathetic adjustment of the race problem.

DRAWING CONCLUSIONS:

1. What does Garvey suggest about efforts by "Negroes" to secure social equality with whites?
2. Why is Garvey critical of the NAACP and W. E. B. DuBois?
3. Why would Garvey's Black Nationalism be appealing to urban, working-class African Americans?

3.4   MADAME C. J. WALKER, 1910S–1960S

Born Sarah Breedlove (1867–1919) in Louisiana, Madame C. J. Walker became one of the most successful Black business owners ever, emerging as an entrepreneurial force during the height of the Jim Crow era. As a widower and single mother to A'Lelia Bundles—who became a leading figure during the Harlem Renaissance of the 1920s—Madame C. J. Walker became a pioneer in hair care and cosmetic products that catered to African Americans. Madame Walker was also an early pioneer in what we would term "wellness" today. Walker built a national corporate empire in Indianapolis, Indiana, that included laboratories, beauty schools, and employed thousands of agents, mostly Black women, across the country. Walker championed civil rights and encouraged her agents to use their power and prestige to do the same. Madame C. J. Walker was also a noted philanthropist and patron of the arts.

GUIDING QUESTIONS:

1. How have African American entrepreneurs supported Black Liberation Movements?
2. What does Madame C. J. Walker's life and legacy teach us about the role of Black women throughout the Black Liberation Movement(s)?
3. Why would hygiene and hair care practices be important topics in the late nineteenth and early twentieth centuries?

IMAGE 7A MADAME C.J. WALKER, 1910S-1960S (1)

From Madam Walker Family Archives, http://madamcjwalker.com/books/#photos

IMAGE 7B MADAME C.J. WALKER, 1910S-1960S (2)

IMAGE 7C MADAME C.J. WALKER, 1910S-1960S (3)

DRAWING CONCLUSIONS:

1. What do these images teach us about Madame C. J. Walker's cosmetics empire?

2. Madame C. J. Walker employed thousands of women agents and encouraged them to build their own business and financial independence. Why is this important, particularly during the Jim Crow era?

3. How does Madame Walker's company reflect the power of the Black Women's Club Movement era?

3.5   ALAIN LOCKE, *THE NEW NEGRO* (1925)

Alain Locke, the first African American Rhodes Scholar and a professor of philosophy at Harvard University, edited a special edition of the magazine *Survey Graphic* in 1925. This special edition focused on life in Harlem, New York. Locke later expanded this into an anthology, *The New Negro*, which became the manifesto of the Harlem Renaissance.

GUIDING QUESTIONS:

1. What does Locke mean by the "New Negro?"
2. What solutions does Locke provide for race problems in the United States?
3. How does Locke see the emergence of the "New Negro" affecting the nation?

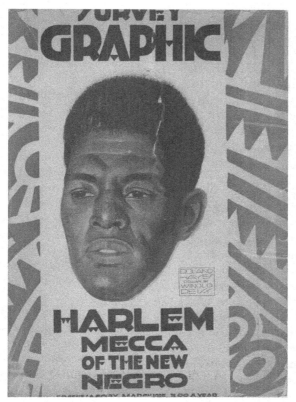

IMAGE 8 SURVEY GRAPHIC, "HARLEM: MECCA OF THE NEW NEGRO" MARCH 1925

Source: Schomburg Center for Research in Black Culture, Manuscripts, Archives and Rare Books Division, The New York Public Library. "Harlem, Mecca of the new Negro. [cover]" New York Public Library Digital Collections. Accessed March 4, 2021. https://digitalcollections.nypl.org/items/510d47df-8dc1-a3d9-e040-e00a18064a99

ALAIN LOCKE, ENTER THE NEW NEGRO

In the last decade something beyond the watch and guard of statistics has happened in the life of the American Negro and the three norms who have traditionally presided over the Negro problem have a changeling in their laps. The Sociologist, The Philanthropist, the Race-leader are not unaware of the New Negro, but they are at a loss to account for him. He simply cannot be swathed in their formulae. For the younger generation is vibrant with a new psychology; the new spirit is awake in the masses, and under the very eyes of the professional observers is transforming what has been a perennial problem into the progressive phases of contemporary Negro life.

Could such a metamorphosis have taken place as suddenly as it has appeared to? The answer is no; not because the New Negro is not here, but because the Old Negro had long become more of a myth than a man. The Old Negro, we must remember, was a creature of moral debate and historical controversy. His has been a stock figure perpetuated as an historical fiction partly in innocent sentimentalism, partly in deliberate reactionism. The Negro himself has contributed his share to this through a sort of protective social mimicry forced upon him by the adverse circumstances of dependence. So for generations in the mind of America, the Negro has been more of a formula than a human being—a something to be argued about, condemned or defended, to be "kept down," or "in his place," or "helped up," to be worried with or worried over, harassed or patronized, a social bogey or a social burden. The thinking Negro even has been induced to share this same general attitude, to focus his attention on controversial issues, to see himself in the distorted perspective of a social problem. His shadow, so to speak, has been more real to him than his personality. Through having had to appeal from the unjust stereotypes of his oppressors and traducers to those of his liberators, friends and benefactors he has subscribed to the traditional positions from which his case has been viewed. Little true social or self-understanding has or could come from such a situation ...

Similarly the mind of the Negro seems suddenly to have slipped from under the tyranny of social intimidation and to be shaking off the psychology of imitation and implied inferiority. By shedding the old chrysalis of the Negro problem we are achieving something like a spiritual emancipation. Until recently, lacking self-understanding, we have been almost as much of a problem to ourselves as we still are to others. But the decade that found us with a problem has left us with only a task. The multitude perhaps feels as yet only a strange relief and a new vague urge, but the thinking few know that in the reaction the vital inner grip of prejudice has been broken.

With this renewed self-respect and self-dependence, the life of the Negro community is bound to enter a new dynamic phase, the buoyancy from within compensating for whatever pressure there may be of conditions from without. The migrant masses, shifting from countryside to city, hurdle several generations of experience at a leap, but more important, the same thing happens spiritually in the life-attitudes and self-expression of the Young Negro, in his poetry, his art, his education and his new outlook, with the additional advantage, of course, of the poise and greater certainty of knowing what it is all about. From this comes the promise and warrant of a new leadership ...

First we must observe some of the changes which since the traditional lines of opinion were drawn have rendered these quite obsolete. A main change has been, of course, that shifting of the Negro population which has made the Negro problem no longer exclusively or even predominantly Southern. Why should our minds remain sectionalized, when the problem itself no longer is? Then the trend of migration has not only been toward the North and the Central Midwest, but city-ward and to the great centers of industry—the problems of adjustment are new, practical, local and not peculiarly racial. Rather they are an integral part of the large industrial and social problems of our present-day democracy. And finally, with the Negro rapidly in process of class differentiation, if it ever was warrantable to regard and treat the Negro en masse, it is becoming with every day less possible, more unjust and more ridiculous ...

For generations the Negro has been the peasant matrix of that section of America which has most undervalued him, and here he has contributed not only materially in labor and in social patience, but spiritually as well. The South has unconsciously absorbed the gift of his folk-temperament. In less than half a generation it will be easier to recognize this, but the fact remains that a leaven of humor, sentiment, imagination and tropic nonchalance has gone into the making of the South from a humble, unacknowledged source. A second crop of the Negro's gifts promises still more largely. He now becomes a conscious contributor and lays aside the status of a beneficiary and ward for that of a collaborator and participant in American civilization. The great social gain in this is the releasing of our talented group from the arid fields of controversy and debate to the productive fields of creative expression. The especially cultural recognition they win should in turn prove the key to that revaluation of the Negro which must precede or accompany any considerable further betterment of race relationships.

But whatever the general effect, the present generation will have added the motives of self-expression and spiritual development to the old and still unfinished task of making material headway and progress. No one who understandingly faces the situation with its substantial accomplishment or views the new scene with its still more abundant promise can be entirely without hope. And certainly, if in our lifetime the Negro should not be able to celebrate his full initiation into American democracy, he can at least, on the warrant of these things, celebrate the attainment of a significant and satisfying new phase of group development, and with it a spiritual Coming of Age.

DRAWING CONCLUSIONS:

1. What is the awakening among African Americans that Locke proclaims?
2. What does Locke state as examples of the ways African Americans have contributed to American society?
3. What does this awakening and the "New Negro" suggest about activism one generation before the Modern Civil Rights Movement of the 1950s and 1960s?

3.6 "STRANGE FRUIT" (1939)

"Strange Fruit" is the iconic song that captured the grotesque practice of lynching. Made famous by blues legend Billie Holiday's rendition, the song brought the horrors of lynching to a national public outside the South, many of whom could only imagine the brutality.

GUIDING QUESTIONS:

1. How does "Strange Fruit" convey the horrors of lynching?
2. Discuss the imagery contained within the lyrics.

Southern trees bear strange fruit
Blood on the leaves and blood at the root
Black bodies swinging in the southern breeze
Strange fruit hanging from the poplar trees

Pastoral scene of the gallant south
The bulging eyes and the twisted mouth
Scent of magnolias, sweet and fresh
Then the sudden smell of burning flesh

Here is fruit for the crows to pluck
For the rain to gather, for the wind to suck
For the sun to rot, for the trees to drop
Here is a strange and bitter crop

DRAWING CONCLUSIONS:

1. How could this song inspire protests against lynching?
2. Listen to a recording on YouTube and discuss the emotions Billie Holiday and the lyrics evoke.

From "Strange Fruit" by Lewis Allan, Maurice Pearl, and Dwayne P. Wiggins (made famous by blues legend Billie Holiday).

3.7 DR. MARTIN LUTHER KING, JR., "ADDRESS TO MONTGOMERY IMPROVEMENT ASSOCIATION," HOLT ST. BAPTIST CHURCH, 1956

As the Montgomery Bus Boycott gained momentum, Rev. Dr. Martin Luther King Jr. gave this speech to a gathering of several thousand people at Holt Street Baptist Church. Among those in attendance were reporters, two television crews, and Black leaders from across Alabama. In the speech, King framed the forthcoming protest in the American democratic tradition and emphasized the need for community involvement for the boycott to be successful.

GUIDING QUESTIONS:

1. How does King's speech highlight the legal questions that shaped the Modern Civil Rights Movement?
2. How does King inject principles of nonviolence into the tactics for the boycott?

My friends, we are certainly very happy to see each of you out this evening. We are here this evening for serious business. (Yes) We are here in a general sense because first and foremost we are American citizens (That's right) and we are determined to apply our citizenship to the fullness of its meaning. (Yeah, That's right) We are here also because of our love for democracy, (Yes) because of our deep-seated belief that democracy transformed from thin paper to thick action (Yes) is the greatest form of government on earth. (That's right)

But we are here in a specific sense, because of the bus situation in Montgomery. (Yes) We are here because we are to get the situation corrected. This situation is not at all new. The problem has existed over endless years. (That's right) For many years now Negroes in Montgomery and so many other areas have been inflicted with the paralysis of crippling fears (Yes) on buses in our community. (That's right) On so many occasions, Negroes have been intimidated and humiliated and impressed-oppressed-because of the sheer fact that they were Negroes. (That's right)

I don't have time this evening to go into the history of these numerous cases. Many of them now are lost in the thick fog of oblivion, (Yes) but at least one stands before us now with glaring dimensions. (Yes)

Just the other day, just last Thursday to be exact, one of the finest citizens in Montgomery (Amen)—not one of the finest Negro citizens (That's right) but one of the finest citizens in Montgomery—was taken from a bus (Yes) and carried to jail and arrested (Yes) because she refused to get up to give her seat to a white person. (Yes, That's right) Now the press would have us believe that she refused to leave a reserved section for Negroes, (Yes) but I want you to know this evening that there is no reserved section. (All right) The law has never been clarified at that point. (Hell no) Now I think I speak with, with legal authority—not that I have any legal authority, but I think I speak with legal authority behind me (All right)—that the law, the ordinance, the city ordinance has never been totally clarified. (That's right)

Mrs. Rosa Parks is a fine person. (Well, well said) And since it had to happen I'm happy that it

From "MIA Mass Meeting at Holt Street Baptist Church," 1955, The Martin Luther King Research and Education Institute, https://kinginstitute.stanford.edu/king-papers/documents/mia-mass-meeting-holt-street-baptist-church

happened to a person like Mrs. Parks, for *nobody can doubt* the boundless outreach of her integrity. (Sure enough) *Nobody can doubt* the height of her character, (Yes) *nobody can doubt* the depth of her Christian commitment and devotion to the teachings of Jesus. (All right) And I'm happy since it had to happen, it happened to a person that nobody can call a disturbing factor in the community. (All right) Mrs. Parks is a fine Christian person, unassuming, and yet there is integrity and character there. And just because she refused to get up, she was arrested.

And you know, my friends, *there comes a time* when people get tired of being trampled over by the iron feet of oppression. [Thundering applause] *There comes a time*, my friends, when people get tired of being plunged across the abyss of humiliation where they experience the bleakness of nagging despair. (Keep talking) *There comes a time* when people get tired of being pushed out of the glittering sunlight of life's July, and left standing amid the piercing chill of an alpine November. (That's right) [Applause] *There comes a time.* (Yes sir, Teach) [Applause continues]

We are here, we are here this evening because we're tired now. (Yes) [Applause] And I want to say, that we are not here advocating violence. (No) We have never done that. (Repeat that, Repeat that) [Applause] I want it to be known throughout Montgomery and throughout this nation (Well) that we are Christian people. (Yes) [Applause] We believe in the Christian religion. We believe in the teachings of Jesus. (Well) The only weapon that we have in our hands this evening is the weapon of protest. (Yes) [Applause] That's all.

And certainly, certainly, this is the glory of America, with all of its faults. (Yeah) This is the glory of our democracy. If we were incarcerated behind the iron curtains of a Communistic nation we couldn't do this. If we were dropped in the dungeon of a totalitarian regime we couldn't do this. (All right) But the great glory of American democracy is the right to protest for right. (That's right) [Applause] My friends, don't let anybody make us feel that we to be compared in our actions with the Ku Klux Klan or with the White Citizens Council. [Applause] There

will be no crosses burned at any bus stops in Montgomery. (Well, That's right) There will be no white persons pulled out of their homes and taken out on some distant road and lynched for not cooperating. [Applause] There will be nobody amid, among us who will stand up and defy the Constitution of this nation. [Applause] We only assemble here because of our desire to see right exist. [Applause] My friends, I want it to be known that we're going to work with grim and bold determination to gain justice on the buses in this city. [Applause]

And we are not wrong, we are not wrong in what we are doing. (Well) If we are wrong, the Supreme Court of this nation is wrong. (Yes sir) [Applause] If we are wrong, the Constitution of the United States is wrong. (Yes) [Applause] If we are wrong, God Almighty is wrong. (That's right) [Applause] If we are wrong, Jesus of Nazareth was merely a utopian dreamer that never came down to earth. (Yes) [Applause] If we are wrong, justice is a lie: (Yes) love has no meaning. [Applause] And we are determined here in Montgomery to work and fight until justice runs down like water (Yes) [Applause] and righteousness like a mighty stream. (Keep talking) [Applause]

I want to say that in all of our actions we must stick together. (That's right) [Applause] Unity is the great need of the hour (Well, That's right) and if we are united we can get many of the things that we not only desire but which we justly deserve. (Yeah) And don't let anybody frighten you. (Yeah) We are not afraid of what we are doing, (Oh no) because we are doing it within the law. (All right) There is never a time in our American democracy that we must ever think we're wrong when we protest. (Yes sir) We reserve that right. When labor all over this nation came to see that it would be trampled over by capitalistic power, it was nothing wrong with labor getting together and organizing and protesting for its rights. (That's right) ...

As we stand and sit here this evening and as we prepare ourselves for what lies ahead, let us go out with a grim and bold determination that we are going to stick together. [Applause] We are going to work together. [Applause] Right here in Montgomery, when the history books are written in the future, (Yes) somebody will have to say, "There lived a race of people, (Well) a black people, (Yes sir) 'fleecy locks and black complexion,' (Yes) a people who had the moral courage to stand up for their rights. [Applause] And thereby they injected a new meaning into the veins of history and of civilization." And we're gonna do that. God grant that we will do it before it is too late. (Oh yeah) As we proceed with our program let us think of these things. (Yes) [Applause]

DRAWING CONCLUSIONS:

1. Before the speech, King considered, "How could I make a speech that would be militant enough to keep my people aroused to positive action and yet moderate enough to keep this fervor within controllable and Christian bounds?" How did King address this balancing act in his speech?

2. What are the key components of the Modern Civil Rights Movement, as outlined in this speech?

3.8   JAMES BALDWIN, "MY DUNGEON SHOOK: LETTER TO MY NEPHEW ON THE ONE HUNDREDTH ANNIVERSARY OF THE EMANCIPATION," 1963

James Baldwin's writings emerged during the heart of the Modern Civil Rights Movement of the 1950s and 1960s. Baldwin's critiques of racism in the United States have garnered ongoing appreciation given how prophetic and incisive these critiques have remained over the last half-century. Baldwin stands as one of the premier intellectuals of race and racism, and embodies the spirit of resistance that has shaped the Black Liberation Movement(s).

GUIDING QUESTIONS:

1. What messages is Baldwin delivering to his nephew?
2. How do these messages reflect past, present, and future challenges facing African Americans?

I have begun this letter five times and torn it up five times. I keep seeing your face, which is also the face of your father and my brother. Like him, you are tough, dark, vulnerable, moody—with a very definite tendency to sound truculent because you want no one to think you are soft. You may be like your grandfather in this, I don't know, but certainly both you and your father resemble him very much physically. Well, he is dead, he never saw you, and he had a terrible life; he was defeated long before he died because, at the bottom of his heart, he really believed what white people said about him. This is one of the reasons that he became so holy. I am sure that your father has told you something about all that. Neither you nor your father exhibit any tendency towards holiness: you really are of another era, part of what happened when the Negro left the land and came into what the late E. Franklin Frazier called "the cities of destruction." You can only be destroyed by believing that you really are what the white world calls a nigger. I tell you this because I love you, and please don't you ever forget it.

I have known both of you all your lives, have carried your Daddy in my arms and on my shoulders, kissed and spanked him and watched him learn to walk. I don't know if you've known anybody from that far back; if you've loved anybody that long, first as an infant, then as a child, then as a man, you gain a strange perspective on time and human pain and effort. Other people cannot see what I see whenever I look into your father's face, for behind your father's face as it is today are all those other faces which were his. Let him laugh and I see a cellar your father does not remember and a house he does not remember and I hear in his present laughter his laughter as a child. Let him curse and I remember him falling down the cellar steps, and howling, and I remember, with pain, his tears, which my hand or your grandmother's so easily wiped away. But no one's hand can wipe away those tears he sheds invisibly today, which one hears in his laughter and in his speech and in his songs. I know what the world has done to my brother and how narrowly he has survived it. And I know,

From James Baldwin, *The Fire Next Time* (New York: Vintage Books, 1963).

which is much worse, and this is the crime of which I accuse my country and my countrymen, and for which neither I nor time nor history will ever forgive them, that they have destroyed and are destroying hundreds of thousands of lives and do not know it and do not want to know it. One can be, indeed one must strive to become, tough and philosophical concerning destruction and death, for this is what most of mankind has been best at since we have heard of man. (But remember: most of mankind is not all of mankind.) But it is not permissible that the authors of devastation should also be innocent. It is the innocence which constitutes the crime.

Now, my dear namesake, these innocent and well-meaning people, your countrymen, have caused you to be born under conditions not very far removed from those described for us by Charles Dickens in the London of more than a hundred years ago. (I hear the chorus of the innocents screaming, "No! This is not true! How bitter you are!"—but I am writing this letter to you, to try to tell you something about how to handle them, for most of them do not yet really know that you exist. I know the conditions under which you were born, for I was there. Your countrymen were not there, and haven't made it yet. Your grandmother was also there, and no one has ever accused her of being bitter. I suggest that the innocents check with her. She isn't hard to find. Your countrymen don't know that she exists, either, though she has been working for them all their lives.)

Well, you were born, here you came, something like fifteen years ago; and though your father and mother and grandmother, looking about the streets through which they were carrying you, staring at the walls into which they brought you, had every reason to be heavyhearted, yet they were not. For here you were, Big James, named for me—you were a big baby, I was not—here you were: to be loved. To be loved, baby, hard, at once, and forever, to strengthen you against the loveless world. Remember that: I know how black it looks today, for you. It looked bad that day, too, yes, we were trembling. We have not stopped trembling yet, but if we had not loved each other none of us would have survived. And now you must survive because we love you, and for the sake of your children and your children's children.

This innocent country set you down in a ghetto in which, in fact, it intended that you should perish. Let me spell out precisely what I mean by that, for the heart of the matter is here, and the root of my dispute with my country. You were born where you were born and faced the future that you faced because you were black and for no other reason. The limits of your ambition were, thus, expected to be set forever. You were born into a society which spelled out with brutal clarity, and in as many ways as possible, that you were a worthless human being. You were not expected to aspire to excellence: you were expected to make peace with mediocrity. Wherever you have turned, James, in your short time on this earth, you have been told where you could go and what you could do (and how you could do it) and where you could live and whom you could marry. I know your countrymen do not agree with me about this, and I hear them saying, "You exaggerate." They do not know Harlem, and I do. So do you. Take no one's word for anything, including mine—but trust your experience. Know whence you came. If you know whence you came, there is really no limit to where you can go. The details and symbols of your life have been deliberately constructed to make you believe what white people say about you. Please try to remember that what they believe, as well as what they do and cause you to endure, does not testify to your inferiority but to their inhumanity and fear. Please try to be clear, dear James, through the storm which rages about your youthful head today, about the reality which lies behind the words acceptance and integration. There is no reason for you to try to become like white people and there is no basis whatever for their impertinent assumption that they must accept you. The really terrible thing, old buddy, is that you must accept them. And I mean that very seriously. You must accept them and accept them with love. For these innocent people have no other hope. They are, in effect, still trapped in a history which they do not understand; and until they understand it, they cannot be released from it. They have had to believe for many years, and for innumerable reasons, that black men are inferior to white men. Many of them, indeed, know better, but, as you will discover, people find it very difficult to act on what they know. To act is to be committed, and to be committed is to be in danger. In this case, the danger, in the minds of most white Americans, is the loss of their identity. Try to imagine how you would feel if you woke up one morning to find the sun shining and all the stars aflame. You would be frightened because it is out of the order of nature. Any upheaval in the universe is terrifying because it so profoundly attacks one's sense of one's own reality. Well, the black man has functioned in the white man's world as a fixed star, as an immovable pillar: and as he moves out of his place, heaven and earth are shaken to their foundations. You, don't be afraid. I said that it was intended that you should perish in the ghetto, perish by never being allowed to go behind the white man's definitions, by never being allowed to spell your proper name. You have, and many of us have, defeated this intention; and, by a terrible law, a terrible paradox, those innocents who believed that your imprisonment made them safe are losing their grasp of reality. But these men are your brothers—your lost, younger brothers. And if the word integration means anything, this is what it means: that we, with love, shall force our brothers to see themselves as they are, to cease fleeing from reality and begin to change it. For this is your home,

my friend, do not be driven from it; great men have done great things here, and will again, and we can make America what America must become. It will be hard, James, but you come from sturdy, peasant stock, men who picked cotton and dammed rivers and built railroads, and, in the teeth of the most terrifying odds, achieved an unassailable and monumental dignity. You come from a long line of great poets, some of the greatest poets since Homer. One of them said, The very time I thought I was lost, My dungeon shook and my chains fell off. You know, and I know, that the country is celebrating one hundred years of freedom one hundred years too soon. We cannot be free until they are free. God bless you, James, and Godspeed.

Your uncle,
James

DRAWING CONCLUSIONS:

1. Why does Baldwin feel compelled to share these thoughts with his nephew?
2. What racial attitudes and are still present nearly sixty years after publication of *The Fire Next Time*?
3. What economic and political challenges, to which Baldwin alludes, remain prevalent today?

3.9 MARCH ON WASHINGTON CORRESPONDENCE AND PROGRAM, 1963

The March on Washington is revered in American history for the organization required to make it possible, the numbers of people in attendance, and the remarkable speeches delivered by Dr. King, Congressman John Lewis, and others. On August 28, a quarter million people convened in Washington, DC, to demand passage for what became the Civil Rights Act of 1964, which brought a formal end to Jim Crow segregation. The following documents trace the behind-the-scenes efforts required to organize and manage an event of this magnitude.

GUIDING QUESTIONS:

1. What were the purposes of the March on Washington?
2. What do these documents teach us about the expertise of the organizing committee?
3. African American women are noticeably absent from the planning committees. Discuss why that was the case.

From "The March on Washington for Jobs and Freedom" (1963), The Center for Legislative Archives, https://www.archives.gov/legislative/features/march-on-washington

NATIONAL ASSOCIATION FOR THE ADVANCEMENT OF COLORED PEOPLE

TWENTY WEST FORTIETH STREET ● NEW YORK, N. Y. 10018 ● BRyant 9-1400

July 30, 1963

TO: PRESIDENTS OF BRANCHES, YOUTH COUNCILS, COLLEGE CHAPTERS AND STATE CONFERENCES

FROM: ROY WILKINS

```
MARCH ON WASHINGTON
A U G U S T    2 8
```

On July 12, I joined with A. Philip Randolph, Whitney M. Young, Jr., Dr. Martin Luther King, Jr., James Farmer, and John Lewis in issuing the Call For A March On Washington For Jobs And Freedom, to take place on Wednesday, August 28, 1963, in Washington, D.C.

I took this action following several weeks of discussion with the other signers and in accord with the policy mandate of our 54th Annual Convention, voted in Chicago on July 2, 1963. IT IS OUR CONSIDERED JUDGMENT THAT THIS PEACEFUL ASSEMBLY AND PETITION IN THE NATION'S CAPITAL IS NOT ONLY IN THE HIGHEST TRADITION OF AMERICAN DEMOCRACY BUT WILL GIVE TREMENDOUS PUSH TO THE PASSAGE OF MEANINGFUL CIVIL RIGHTS BILLS IN THIS SESSION OF CONGRESS.

The March on Washington for Jobs and Freedom MUST HAVE the support and participation of every American, black or white, who genuinely wants civil rights and who can manage in some way to come to Washington. No less than 100,000 of us MUST BE ON HAND that morning.

An experienced staff has been assembled to develop and carry out the plans for the March. The NAACP has contributed money and has assigned a full-time staff member to the March. The Assistant to the Executive Secretary is a member of the March administrative committee. The Director of Branches is a consultant to the committee. NAACP staff vacations have, in many cases, been cancelled for the summer and in other cases they have been curtailed. All vacationing staff members are subject to recall on 24-hour notice. And this is not only for the March: this is for the duration of the civil rights battle in the Congress.

It is impossible for me to overemphasize the vital part which the NAACP branches and members must play if the March is to bring us the results we seek. To a very great extent, the March will move or drag depending upon what YOU, as an NAACP leader, do for it.

I am enclosing a copy of the Organizing Manual for the March. This contains almost all the information you will need in order to go to work to promote a huge attendance from your city. PLEASE READ IT CAREFULLY AND UNDERSTAND IT. Especially, note the back page, on which are listed the promotional materials which you can order — in whatever quantity you need — from the March Headquarters, at 170 West 130 Street, New York 27, N.Y.

Besides the action your branch takes, there should be close liaison and cooperation across your community, so that no interested person is left out. You may find it useful to take the lead in setting up a special March Committee in your community, to facilitate planning for buses, trains, or other means of getting the biggest possible group to Washington.

We will continue to send you word on developments as they come about.

LET'S GO! ALL OUT FOR THE MARCH ON WASHINGTON FOR JOBS AND FREEDOM, AUGUST 28, 1963.

```
                        U R G E N T
THE NAACP LEGISLATIVE CONFERENCE AUGUST 6-8 TO WHICH YOU HAVE BEEN
REQUESTED TO SEND DELEGATES FROM EACH CONGRESSIONAL DISTRICT IN YOUR
COMMUNITY IS A NECESSARY FORERUNNER TO THE MARCH ON AUGUST 28. IT
IS ESSENTIAL THAT EVERY NAACP BRANCH PARTICIPATE IN BOTH ACTIVITIES.
```

RW:crn
Encl.

IMAGE 10A MARCH ON WASHINGTON CORRESPONDENCE AND PROGRAM, 1963 (1)

Wednesday August 28, 1963

MARCH ON WASHINGTON FOR JOBS AND FREEDOM

170 West 130 Street
New York 27, New York
FIlmore 8-1900

August 18, 1963

Founding Chairmen
Mathew Ahmann
Eugene Carson Blake
James Farmer
Martin Luther King
John Lewis
Joachin Prinz
A. Philip Randolph
Walter Reuther
Roy Wilkins
Whitney Young

Administrative Committee
Cleveland Robinson
Chairman
Courtland Cox
Ann Arnold Hedgeman
Rev. Thomas Kilgore, Jr.
Rev. George Lawrence
James McCain
Gloster Current
Guichard Parris
Erwin Suall

Director
A. Philip Randolph

Deputy Director
Bayard Rustin

Coordinators
Norman Hill
L. Joseph Overton

Southern Administrators
Dr. Aaron Henry
Worth Long
Att. Floyd McKissick
Rev. Wyatt Walker

Mr. Stokley Carmichael
Student Nonviolent Coordinating Committee
708 Avenue N
Greenwood, Mississippi

Dear Stokley,

I have gone to great lengths to inquire as to the possibilities of providing transportation for the people from the Southern areas, let me tell you partner ain't nothing happening.

Frank Monter, the late fund raiser for the March now working for the U.N., states that there was a slight misunderstanding as to the promise for those fifty buses.

Both of the "Freedom Trains" have been abandoned. There are five coaches being chartered from Birmingham which is now alleged to be the "Freedom Train". There will also be a few buses from here and there, the largest number coming from the upper South (e.g. North Carolina, Virginia).

You know the old saying, in Harlem that goes, "I feels for you brother but I can't reach you." This seems to be exactly the case as far as our brothers down home are concerned.

Everyday I am caught by a fit of depression because of the almost unconcerned attitude of those who are able to underwrite the cost for the trains from the South (e.g. NAACP, SCLC).

Bayard proposed that if the two organizations would take responsibility for the trains the March Committee would raise the funds after the March to assure that no loss is incurred. Their reply...nothing doing.

You know good buddy when Billie Holiday said "Mama (NAACP) may have and Papa (SCLC) may have but God bless the child (the sharecropper) that got its own, that's got it's own, she wasn't funning.

Yours respectfully,

Courtland Cox

IMAGE 10B MARCH ON WASHINGTON CORRESPONDENCE AND PROGRAM, 1963 (2)

MEMORANDUM

August 22, 1963

TO: Bayard
FROM: Courtland Cox
RE: Transportation

THE SOUTH

Virginia:

Buses

1 Charlotte
3 Lynchburg
13 Richmond
2 Petersburg
6 Norfolk
2 Newport News
2 Chatham
1 Danville

total.....20

Mississippi:

Buses

3 Jackson
2 Greenwood
1 Gulfport
1 Clarksdale

total..... 7

Georgia:

Buses

7 Atlanta
2 Macon
3 Albany
total.....11
Trains

1 Albany (100/ people)
  Savannah (200/ ")

total.....550 people

North Carolina

Buses

22 Durham
2 Greensboro
total.....25
1 Monroe

Maryland:

Buses

2 Cambridge
50 Baltimore
2 Annapolis
total.....54

Texas:

Buses

3
total.....3

Oklahoma:

Buses

2
total.....2

Louisiana:

Buses

1 Baton Rouge
1 New Orleans
total.....2

Arkansas:

Buses

5
total.....5

Tennessee:
Buses

2 Nashville
4 Chatanooga
4 Memphis and
  other areas

total.....10

South Carolina:
Buses

S. Carolina (con't)

Trains

4 coaches
Sumter 122 people
Charleston 200 "

total.....325/

West Virginia:

ten carloads-Charleston

Florida:

Trains

2 coaches-Jacksonville
1 coach -Florence

total.....150 people

Alabama:

Buses

6 Birmingham
1 Montgomery
1 Selma

total.....8

Kentucky:

250 people expected

TOTAL..... 7,000

IMAGE 10C MARCH ON WASHINGTON CORRESPONDENCE AND
PROGRAM, 1963 (3)

Wednesday August 28, 1963

MARCH ON WASHINGTON FOR JOBS AND FREEDOM

170 West 130 Street

New York 27, New York

FIlmore 8-1900

MEMO

Founding Chairmen
James Farmer
Martin Luther King
John Lewis
A. Philip Randolph
Roy Wilkins
Whitney Young

Administrative Committee
Cleveland Robinson
  Chairman
Courtland Cox
Ann Arnold Hedgeman
Rev. Thomas Kilgore, Jr.
Rev. George Lawrence
James McCain
Dr. John Morsell
Guichard Parris

Director
A. Philip Randolph

Deputy Director
Bayard Rustin

Coordinators
Norman Hill
L. Joseph Overton

Southern Administrators
Dr. Aaron Henry
Worth Long
Att. Floyd McKissick
Rev. Wyatt Walker

To: Bayard
From: Courtland
R$_e$: Southern Freedom Trains

I have communicated with the various railroads asking for
a written reply which would give the reasons for the lack
of the transportation facilities for the March. I also
included in the letter a statement concerning our inten-
tions to send copies of their letters to the I. C. C.

When they send their replies I suggest that a statement
be released to the press and/or a telegram to Robert
Kennedy stating the following:

1) Participants will be travelling through the South for
   long distances and much of the travelling will be done
   at night through areas that have been known to be dangerous for travel when buses or cars transporting
   Negroes or an integrated group have risked travelling
   through these areas.

2) If we are not able to secure the transportation facilities of the railroads we have no choice but to use
   buses and cars for transportation to Washington.

3) The possibility of injury to our participants is therefore greatly increased and if this possibility becomes
   a reality, as we know it will, the United States government would be placed in a very embarassing and dangerous
   position.

4) Therefore, we are asking that you inform the railroads
   as to the possible dangers involved in not making
   trains available to the March Committee.

P. S. You might call Martin King and ask him
if he has secured the train from Coastline
railroad. If he has not impress upon him the
importance of reserving that train.

IMAGE 10D MARCH ON WASHINGTON CORRESPONDENCE AND PROGRAM, 1963 (4)

MARCH ON WASHINGTON FOR JOBS AND FREEDOM
AUGUST 28, 1963

LINCOLN MEMORIAL PROGRAM

1. The National Anthem	*Led by* Marian Anderson.
2. Invocation	The Very Rev. Patrick O'Boyle, *Archbishop of Washington.*
3. Opening Remarks	A. Philip Randolph, *Director March on Washington for Jobs and Freedom.*
4. Remarks	Dr. Eugene Carson Blake, *Stated Clerk, United Presbyterian Church of the U.S.A.; Vice Chairman, Commission on Race Relations of the National Council of Churches of Christ in America.*

5. Tribute to Negro Women Fighters for Freedom
  Daisy Bates
  Diane Nash Bevel
  Mrs. Medgar Evers
  Mrs. Herbert Lee
  Rosa Parks
  Gloria Richardson
	Mrs. Medgar Evers

6. Remarks	John Lewis, *National Chairman, Student Nonviolent Coordinating Committee.*
7. Remarks	Walter Reuther, *President, United Automobile, Aerospace and Agricultural Implement Wokers of America, AFL-CIO; Chairman, Industrial Union Department, AFL-CIO.*
8. Remarks	James Farmer, *National Director, Congress of Racial Equality.*
9. Selection	Eva Jessye *Choir*
10. Prayer	Rabbi Uri Miller, *President Synagogue Council of America.*
11. Remarks	Whitney M. Young, Jr., *Executive Director, National Urban League.*
12. Remarks	Mathew Ahmann, *Executive Director, National Catholic Conference for Interracial Justice.*
13. Remarks	Roy Wilkins, *Executive Secretary, National Association for the Advancement of Colored People.*
14. Selection	Miss Mahalia Jackson
15. Remarks	Rabbi Joachim Prinz, *President American Jewish Congress.*
16. Remarks	The Rev. Dr. Martin Luther King, Jr., *President, Southern Christian Leadership Conference.*
17. The Pledge	A Philip Randolph
18. Benediction	Dr. Benjamin E. Mays, *President, Morehouse College.*

"WE SHALL OVERCOME"

IMAGE 10E MARCH ON WASHINGTON CORRESPONDENCE AND PROGRAM, 1963 (5)

DRAWING CONCLUSIONS:

1. What concerns are raised in the correspondence?
2. Who spoke at the March on Washington?

3. Discuss the roles African American women played during this era, and consider the impact of leading Black women organizers, such as Ella Baker, Dianne Nash, and Fannie Lou Hamer.

3.10   MALCOLM X, "BALLOT OR THE BULLET," KING SOLOMON BAPTIST CHURCH, DETROIT, MICHIGAN, APRIL 12, 1964

By 1964, Malcolm X had left the Nation of Islam (NOI) and was in the process of reshaping his own political ideologies independent of Elijah Muhammad and his teachings as the leader of the NOI. However, a year later Malcolm was assassinated before his full platform could mature. In this speech, we see the early stages of Malcolm's political philosophies, which are incomplete given his untimely death.

GUIDING QUESTIONS:

1. What are Malcolm's emerging philosophies?
2. How does Malcolm define Black Nationalism?
3. Who is Malcolm's audience?

Mr. Moderator, Rev. Cleage, brothers and sisters and friends, and I see some enemies. *[laughter, applause]* In fact, I think we'd be fooling ourselves if we had an audience this large and didn't realize that there were some enemies present.

This afternoon we want to talk about the ballot or the bullet. The ballot or the bullet explains itself. But before we get into it, since this is the year of the ballot or the bullet, I would like to clarify some things that refer to me personally, concerning my own personal position.

I'm still a Muslim. That is, my religion is still Islam. *[applause]* My religion is still Islam. I still credit Mr. Muhammad for what I know and what I am. He's the one who opened my eyes. *[applause]* At present I am the minister of the newly founded Muslim Mosque Incorporated, which has its offices in the Theresa Hotel right in the heart of Harlem, that's the black belt in New York City ...

I am a Muslim minister. The same as they are Christian ministers, I'm a Muslim minister. And I don't believe in fighting today on any one front, but on all fronts. *[applause]* In fact, I'm a Black Nationalist freedom fighter. *[applause]* Islam is my religion but I believe my religion is my personal business. *[applause]*

So today, though Islam is my religious philosophy, my political, economic and social philosophy is black nationalism.... . The political philosophy of black nationalism only means that the black man should control the politics and the politicians in his own community.... . The political philosophy of black nationalism only means that if you and I are going to live in a black community— ... We must, we must understand the politics of our community and we must know what politics is supposed to produce. We must know what part politics play in our lives. And until we become politically mature, we will always be misled, led astray, or deceived or maneuvered into supporting someone politically who doesn't have the good of our community at heart. So the political philosophy of black nationalism only means that we will have to carry on a program, a political program, of reeducation—to open our people's eyes, make us become more politically conscious, politically mature. And then, we will—whenever we are ready to cast our ballot, that ballot will be cast for a man of

From *American Radio Works: Say It Plain, Say It Loud; A Century of Great African America Speeches*, http://americanradioworks. publicradio.org/features/blackspeech/mx.html

the community, who has the good of the community at heart. *[applause]*

The economic philosophy of black nationalism only means that we should own and operate and control the economy of our community ... the economic philosophy of black nationalism only means that we have to become involved in a program of reeducation, to educate our people into the importance of knowing that when you spend your dollar out of the community in which you live, the community in which you spend your money becomes richer and richer, the community out of which you take your money becomes poorer and poorer. And because these Negroes, who have been misled, misguided, are breaking their necks to take their money and spend it with the Man, the Man is becoming richer and richer, and you're becoming poorer and poorer. And then what happens? The community in which you live becomes a slum. It becomes a ghetto. The conditions become rundown. And then you have the audacity to complain about poor housing in a rundown community, while you're running down yourselves when you take your dollar out. *[applause]*

Why does it look like it might be the year of the ballot or the bullet? Because Negroes have listened to the trickery and the lies and the false promises of the white man now for too long, and they're fed up. They've become disenchanted. They've become disillusioned. They've become dissatisfied. And all of this has built up frustrations in the black community that makes the black community throughout America today more explosive than all of the atomic bombs the Russians can ever invent. Whenever you got a racial powder keg sitting in your lap, you're in more trouble than if you had an atomic powder keg sitting in your lap. When a racial powder keg goes off, it doesn't care who it knocks out the way. Understand this, it's dangerous... .

So today our people are disillusioned ... And in 1964 you'll see this young black man, this new generation, asking for the ballot or the bullet. That old Uncle Tom action is outdated. The young generation don't want to hear anything about "the odds are against us." What do we care about odds? *[applause]*

... Why is America—why does this loom to be such an explosive political year? Because this is the year of politics. This is the year when all of the white politicians are going to come into the Negro community. You never see them until election time. You can't find them until election time. *[applause]* They're going to come in with false promises. And as they make these false promises they're going to feed our frustrations, and this will only serve to make matters worse. I'm no politician. I'm not even a student of politics. I'm not a Republican, nor a Democrat, nor an American—and got sense enough to know it. *[applause]*

... You're the one who has that power. You can keep Johnson in Washington D.C., or you can send him back to his Texas cotton patch. *[applause]* You're the one who sent Kennedy to Washington. You're the one who put the present Democratic administration in Washington, D.C. The whites were evenly divided. It was the fact that you threw 80 percent of your votes behind the Democrats that put the Democrats in the White House ...

... Any time you throw your weight behind a political party that controls two-thirds of the government, and that party can't keep the promise that it made to you during election-time, and you're dumb enough to walk around continuing to identify yourself with that party, you're not only a chump but you're a traitor to your race. *[applause]*

Oh, I say you been misled. You been had. You been took. *[laughter, applause]*...

This is why I say it's the ballot or the bullet. It's liberty or it's death. It's freedom for everybody or freedom for nobody. *[applause]*

... So those of us whose political and economic and social philosophy is black nationalism have become involved in the civil rights struggle. We have injected ourselves into the civil rights struggle. And we intend to expand it from the level of civil rights to the level of human rights. As long as you fight it on the level of civil rights, you're under Uncle Sam's jurisdiction. You're going to his court expecting him to correct the problem. He created the problem. He's the criminal! You don't take your case to the criminal, you take your criminal to court. *[applause]*

... Now you tell me how can the plight of everybody on this Earth reach the halls of the United Nations and you have twenty-two million Afro-Americans whose churches are being bombed, whose little girls are being murdered, whose leaders are being shot down in broad daylight?

... So our next move is to take the entire civil rights struggle—problem—into the United Nations and let the world see that Uncle Sam is guilty of violating the human rights of 22 million Afro-Americans right down to the year of 1964 and still has the audacity or the nerve to stand up and represent himself as the leader of the free world? *[cheering]* Not only is he a crook, he's a hypocrite. Here he is standing up in front of other people, Uncle Sam, with the blood of your and mine mothers and fathers on his hands. With the blood dripping down his jaws like a bloody-jawed wolf. And still got the nerve to point his finger at other countries. In 1964 you can't even get civil rights legislation and this man has got the nerve to stand up and talk about South Africa or talk about Nazi Germany or talk about Portugal. No, no more days like those! *[applause]*

So I say in my conclusion, the only way we're going to solve it: we got to unite. We got to work together in unity and harmony. And black nationalism is the key ...

DRAWING CONCLUSIONS:

1. Why is this speech titled "The Ballot or the Bullet"?
2. Why does Malcolm as a political figure continue to resonate generations later?
3. Make comparisons and contrasts with Marcus Garvey's platform for the UNIA.
4. Why was Malcolm seemingly able to predict the urban riots and rebellions of the mid-sixties?

3.11 ELLA BAKER, "ADDRESS AT THE HATTIESBURG FREEDOM DAY RALLY," 1964

Ella Josephine Baker was one of the most revered civil and human rights activists and organizers across the twentieth century's Black Liberation Movement(s). Born in 1903, Baker was raised in North Carolina and graduated from Shaw University (Raleigh, NC) as valedictorian of her class. Baker's career extended for over five decades during which she championed grassroots radicalism and mentored many younger activists, most notably serving as advisor during the formation of the Student Nonviolent Coordinating Committee. Baker was also critical of sexism within the ranks of civil rights leadership.

GUIDING QUESTIONS:
1. What is the cause which Baker states she works for?
2. What human rights does Baker explain as being central to true "freedom?"

[1] This is rather unusual. Aaron Henry said that I had had my fling with all the civil rights organizations. Well, my greatest fling has still to be flung, because as far as I'm concerned I was never working for an organization, I have always tried to work for a cause, and the cause to me is bigger than any organization. Bigger than any group of people, and it is the cause of humanity. The cause is the cause that brings us together, the drive of the human spirit for freedom.

[2] You know, I always like to think that the very God who gave us life, gave us liberty. And if we don't have liberty it is because somebody else has stood between us and that which God has granted us. And so we have come here tonight to renew our struggle, our struggle for that which we are entitled by virtue of being children of the Almighty. The right to be men and women, to grow and to develop to the fullest capacity with which He has endowed us.

[3] And as I have listened here tonight, my spirit has rove over a long period of years and I can think of a number of things I would like to say, but if I had anything at all to say tonight is to remind us of something that occurred to me, something that came into focus in a conversation on the night that Medger Evers's body came through Atlanta. A group of people were down at the station among us; we were there for the purpose of identifying with the great tragedy that had occurred in his being shot to death. And after the ceremony, the little ceremony in the station, one of the leading civil right leaders (I won't name any because leadership is one of those things, you know, I won't talk about them too much) but this person said, "We are in the final stages of the freedom struggle." And I challenge that.

[4] We are not in the final stages of the freedom struggle. We are really just beginning. We are just beginning the freedom struggle. Let me tell you why. Because even tomorrow if every vestige of racial discrimination were wiped out, if all of us became free enough to go down and to associate with all the people we wanted to associate, we still are not free. We aren't free until within us we have that deep sense of freedom from a lot of things that we don't even mention in these meetings.

From Voices of Democracy: The U.S. Oratory Project, https://voicesofdemocracy.umd.edu/ella-baker-freedom-day-rally-speech-text/

[5] And I'm not talking about Negroes, I'm talking about people. People cannot be free until they realize that peace—we can talk about peace—that peace is not the absence of war or struggle, it is the presence of justice. People cannot, pardon me, people cannot be free until there is enough work in the land to give everybody a job. Tomorrow, tomorrow if we were able to vote our full strength and we still voted our full strength, until we recognize that in this country in a land of great and plenty and great wealth there are millions of people who go to bed hungry every night. That tomorrow if we were to call up all the able-bodied men in our country, who could do some work, we wouldn't have work for them to do.

[6] And unless we see this thing in its larger perspective, unless we realize that certainly we must sing, we must have the inspiration of song, the inspiration that comes from songs like this one that was created and demonstrated here tonight, but we also must have the information that comes from lots and lots of study. And so we must come to grips with a lot of problems. We must also know that we are in, in the final analysis, the only group that can make your free is yourself, because we must free ourselves from all of things that keep us back.

[7] And so in conclusion let me quote one of my favorite or improvise one of my favorite thoughts in scripture. And it has to do with the whole struggle I think because it says, "For now we are nearer than when we first believed." I forgot the exact quote, but let us "cast aside the works of darkness and put on the armor of light."

[8] I love to hear us sing. I've heard a lot of singing in my day. I've been a part of a lot of singing, but I know, and you must know, that singing alone will not do it for us. And we are going to have to have these freedom schools and we are going to have to

learn a lot of things in them. We are going to have to be concerned about the kinds of education our children are getting in school, and all of this has to be done along at the same time that we also recognize that our white brothers, the very white brothers in Hattiesburg and in other parts of Mississippi who have kept us in bondage, that they did it because they did not know any better.

[9] They have been fooled, and they have been fooled by those who told them the "big lie." The "big lie" was to the effect that they could do what they wanted in Mississippi with the Negro question. And you know what? The rest of the country for a long time tacitly agreed. That is, they didn't do anything about it.

[10] And so all of us stand guilty at this moment for having waited so long to lend ourselves to a fight for the freedom, not of Negroes, not of the Negroes of Mississippi, but for the freedom of the American spirit, for the freedom of the human spirit for freedom, and this is the reason I am here tonight, and this is the reason, I think, that these young men who have worked and given their bodies in the movement for freedom. They are here not because they want to see something take place just for the fun of it, they are here because they should know, and I think they do know, that the freedom which they seek is a larger freedom that encompasses all mankind. And until that day, we will never turn back.

DRAWING CONCLUSIONS:

1. What are the rights that Ella Baker discusses in this speech?

2. How important are employment, education, and housing to meaningful definitions of freedom and equality?

3. Why does Baker say, "We are just beginning the freedom struggle"?

3.12 THE BLACK PANTHER PARTY FOR SELF-DEFENSE PLATFORM, 1966

The Black Panther Party for Self-Defense signifies the Black Power movement and emerging radicalism of the 1960s. While history and memory will forever link the group with their embracing of the Second Amendment, their dismantling led by FBI's Counter Intelligence Program (COINTELPRO), and their infamous skirmishes with the police, historians also highlight the impact of their social programming and the critical leadership women of the Party provided in the administering of those programs. The Black Panther Party platform highlights the group's radicalism as the 1960s folded into the 1970s.

GUIDING QUESTIONS:

1. How does the Black Panther Party platform depart from the southern civil rights movement agenda?
2. Why does the Black Panther Party platform link its "Wants" and "Beliefs" to the Declaration of Independence?

WHAT WE WANT

WHAT WE BELIEVE

1. *We want freedom. We want power to determine the destiny of our Black Community.*
   We believe that black people will not be free until we are able to determine our destiny.
2. *We want full employment for our people.*
   We believe that the federal government is responsible and obligated to give every man employment or a guaranteed income. We believe that if the white American businessmen will not give full employment, then the means of production should be taken from the businessmen and placed in the community so that the people of the community can organize and employ all of its people and give a high standard of living.
3. *We want an end to the robbery by the white man of our Black Community.*
   We believe that this racist government has robbed us and now we are demanding the overdue debt of forty acres and two mules. Forty acres and two mules was promised 100 years ago as restitution for slave labor and mass murder of black people. We will accept the payment as currency which will be distributed to our many communities. The Germans are now aiding the Jews in Israel for the genocide of the Jewish people. The Germans murdered six million Jews. The American racist has taken part in the slaughter of over twenty million black people; therefore, we feel that this is a modest demand that we make.
4. *We want decent housing, fit for shelter of human beings.*
   We believe that if the white landlords will not give decent housing to our black community, then the housing and the land should be made into cooperatives so that our community, with government aid, can build and make decent housing for its people.
5. *We want education for our people that exposes the true nature of this decadent American society. We want education that teaches us our true history and our role in the present-day society.*

From Black Lives Matter Syllabus, http://www.blacklivesmattersyllabus.com/wp-content/uploads/2016/07/BPP_Ten_Point_Program.pdf

We believe in an educational system that will give to our people a knowledge of self. If a man does not have knowledge of himself and his position in society and the world, then he has little chance to relate to anything else.

6. *We want all black men to be exempt from military service.*

   We believe that Black people should not be forced to fight in the military service to defend a racist government that does not protect us. We will not fight and kill other people of color in the world who, like black people, are being victimized by the white racist government of America. We will protect ourselves from the force and violence of the racist police and the racist military, by whatever means necessary.

7. *We want an immediate end to police brutality and murder of black people.*

   We believe we can end police brutality in our black community by organizing black self-defense groups that are dedicated to defending our black community from racist police oppression and brutality. The Second Amendment to the Constitution of the United States gives a right to bear arms. We therefore believe that all black people should arm themselves for self-defense.

8. *We want freedom for all black men held in federal, state, county and city prisons and jails.*

   We believe that all black people should be released from the many jails and prisons because they have not received a fair and impartial trial.

9. *We want all black people when brought to trial to be tried in court by a jury of their peer group or people from their black communities, as defined by the Constitution of the United States.*

   We believe that the courts should follow the United States Constitution so that black people will receive fair trials. The 14th Amendment of the U.S. Constitution gives a man a right to be tried by his peer group. A peer is a person from a similar economic, social, religious, geographical, environmental, historical and racial background. To do this the court will be forced to select a jury from the black community from which the black defendant came. We have been, and are being tried by all-white juries that have no understanding of the "average reasoning man" of the black community.

10. *We want land, bread, housing, education, clothing, justice and peace. And as our major political objective, a United Nations–supervised plebiscite to be held throughout the black colony in which only black colonial subjects will be allowed to participate for the purpose of determining the will of black people as to their national destiny.*

When in the course of human events, it becomes necessary for one people to dissolve the political bands which have connected them with another, and to assume, among the powers of the earth, the separate and equal station to which the laws of nature and nature's God entitle them, a decent respect to the opinions of mankind requires that they should declare the causes which impel them to the separation.

We hold these truths to be self-evident, that all men are created equal; that they are endowed by their Creator with certain unalienable rights; that among these are life, liberty, and the pursuit of happiness. *That, to secure these rights, governments are instituted among men, deriving their just powers from the consent of the governed; that, whenever any form of government becomes destructive of these ends, it is the right of the people to alter or to abolish it, and to institute a new government, laying its foundation on such principles, and organizing its powers in such form, as to them shall seem most likely to effect their safety and happiness.* Prudence, indeed, will dictate that governments long established should not be changed for light and transient causes; and accordingly, all experience hath shown, that mankind are more disposed to supper, while evils are sufferable, than to right themselves by abolishing the forms to which they are accustomed. *But, when a long train of abuses and usurpations, pursuing invariable the same object, evinces a design to reduce them under absolute despotism, it is their right, it is their duty, to throw off such government, and to provide new guards for their future security.*

DRAWING CONCLUSIONS:

1. Which of the ten points remains an issue today?
2. Which of the ten points seems achievable today?

3.13 REPRESENTATIVE SHIRLEY CHISOLM, "SPEECH AT HOWARD UNIVERSITY," 1969 (EXCERPTS)

Representative Shirley Chisolm, born in Brooklyn, New York, became the first Black woman elected to Congress in 1968 and the first Black candidate to seek a major party nomination for President of the United States in 1972. Under the credo "Unbought and Unbossed," Chisolm served in Congress for fourteen years and was a founding member of the Congressional Black Caucus in 1971. Representative Chisolm was an ardent supporter of racial and gender equality, outspoken in her pride of being both Black and a woman.

GUIDING QUESTIONS:

1. What does Rep. Chisolm determine is central to demands for Black liberation?
2. What does Rep. Chisolm state about the call to return to Africa?
3. What does Rep. Chisolm suggest about the meaning of Black Power?

Thank you very much for that wonderful introduction. Good afternoon, students …

The United States can no longer afford the luxury of costly morally, religiously, and ethically wrong racial discrimination. For America needs all of her citizens with their abilities developed to make a fuller contribution to the future. Many problems scream loudly in this country. The thousands of black citizens disenfranchised, living under degrading conditions. The millions of poor in this nation, white and black, who lack the bare rudiments for fruitful living. The rapidly growing numbers of children caught in a web of disillusionment which destroys their will to learn. The increasing numbers of aged who do not even look forward to rest or retirement.

And despite the historic legislation in our cities and our states, nearly eleven million black citizens today still live in basic ghetto communities of our cities. From decades of non-participation, or only modest participation, the black man has within the last two years shifted his goal to full political participation for full American citizenship. And while on the picket line at the lunch counter and on the bus and the store boycott the black man came face to face with the full breadth and weight of the power of influence exercised by local and state governments intertwining and often stifling the protests.

Indeed, a principle byproduct of the American Civil Rights Movement has been the awakening of the black citizen to his awesome political potential. And just as the picket line and the lunch counter demonstrations and the boycotts were dramatic and effective weapons of protest for the civil rights movement, the polling place is the new phase in the new thrust of the black man's bid for equality of opportunity …

… The leaders of today in the black communities must be able to place the goal of freedom ahead of personal ambition. The truly dedicated leader follows what his conscience tells him is best for his people.

From American Radio Works, *Say It Plain, Say It Loud: A Century of Great African American Speeches*, http://americanradioworks. publicradio.org/features/blackspeech/schisholm-2.html

For whatever else the black man is, he is American. Or whatever he is to become integrated, unintegrated, or disintegrated he will become it in America. Only a minority of black people have ever succumbed to the temptation to seek greener pastures of another country or another ideology. You know, so often nowadays we hear people say that we should go back to Africa, we should establish ourselves in Africa, or we should do a lot of other things.

Well if people want to go back to Africa or people want to go to Africa just like people want to go to Europe, that's their own personal business. And you do it voluntarily. I don't intend to go to Africa, I intend to stay here and fight because the blood, sweat, and tears of our forefathers are rooted in the soil of this country. And the reason that Wall Street is the great financial center that it is today is because of the blood sweat and tears of your forefathers who worked in the tobacco and the cotton fields …

… Now that we are beginning to do what they have been telling us to do for a long time, take ourselves up by our bootstraps and begin to consolidate our efforts and move out like every other group has moved out in America. Everybody is so hysterical and panic stricken because of the adjective that precedes the word power: "black." You know it would have been hoped in this country that we would never have to use the word "black" before the word "power" because America has been built on series of immigrants coming into this land rising up and moving out in terms of achieving power to control their lives …

And Black people will gain only as much as they can through their ability to organize independent bases of economic and political power. Through boycotts, electoral activity, rent strikes, etcetera. Black power is concerned with organizing the rage of black people. Organizing the rage. And is putting new hard questions and demands to white America. We will build a new sense of community among our people. We will foster a bond between those who have made it and those on the bottom.

… Let me say to you, my brothers and sisters, that until we can organize to create black unity with an economic base. Until we can develop a plan for action to achieve the goals to make us totally independent and not have to look to the man in order to live, we are not liberated. We must become doers and producers in the system in order to be able to control our own destinies. We have the potential, but we must consolidate all of our strength for eventual liberation …

We need a liberated and developing black community in America that once it has fully discovered it's inherent worth and power, turns to the even greater task of protecting and enlarging upon it's triumphs by further enriching an American culture that already has drawn so much from the black life stream. We need black businessmen who can rise beyond the local tax and spend and make dollars as well as cents for a black community that plays a full part in all levels of government. And there can be no understanding of the recent rioting of northern black ghettos or any realistic analysis of its impact upon the civil rights movement in the nation, without the realization that black citizens have just pressing and long neglected grievances.

We do not erupt simply for exercise. We do not curse imaginary obstacles and procedures. Our resentments are not the product of a momentary flare-up, but of years of postponement, denial, insult, and abuse. The conscience of political democracy cries out for an end to false democracy. It has just been inevitable that black Americans are tired of being governed by laws they had no part in making. And by officials in who's choice they have no voice. It is idiotic to labor under the old the white supremacist supposition: that a white man knows what's good for the black man.

The non-white American is saying, "We no longer want tokens which will only take us on a subway ride. We want some bread, some meat, and a slice, not a sliver pie, the same way any other ethnic group receives under this system." In humanitarian terms, the war on poverty must be fought wherever it is found. Part of the battle must be fought with the establishment of the hundred dollars per week minimum for all Americans so that subsidation by welfare authorities is drastically reduced. And a man is paid a decent living wage in today's automated society. In today's most affluent society, if you please. The goal must be

$2.50 per hour. A national minimum for all Americans. This reduces poverty.

More crassly put, we will be able to get more people off welfare and relief roles, and on to tax roles. we can get them out of the alleys of society and into the mainstream of productive society and productive employment where they can support themselves and their dependents with dignity and pride. Where they can contribute to the growth and strength of the nation's economy.

DRAWING CONCLUSIONS:

1. Compare Rep. Chisolm's argument about Black liberation to Garvey's or Malcolm X's definitions of Black Nationalism. What is similar and different about each?

2. What does Rep. Chisolm mean by a "false democracy?"

3. Compare a living wage and minimum wage in 1969 to today. How has the amount changed? Is either amount truly livable, then or now?

3.14 DR. ANGEL DAVIS, EXCERPT FROM "SPEECH DELIVERED AT THE EMBASSY AUDITORIUM," 1972

Dr. Angela Davis was born in 1944 in Birmingham, Alabama, and witnessed the racial terror that defined the Jim Crow South. A self-proclaimed communist and brilliant intellectual, Dr. Davis became synonymous with Black radicalism in the 1970s. Davis's imprint as a scholar and activists continues to shape the intellectual foundations and the functional applications of Black liberation over five decades into her career.

GUIDING QUESTIONS:

1. Why did Dr. Angela Davis point out prisons and policing as a new frontier for the Black Liberation Movement(s)?
2. How does Dr. Davis's speech capture the spirit of radicalism during the Black Power era?

It's really a wonderful feeling to be back among the people. *[applause, cheers]* To be back among all of you who fought so long and so hard, among all of you who actually achieved my freedom. And I really wish you could have been there in the courtroom at the moment when those three "not guilty" verdicts were pronounced, because that victory was just as much yours as it was mine …

And in the midst of all of this it's sort of difficult for me to grasp that I am the person around whom all of this enthusiasm has emerged. Yet because of it I feel that I have a special responsibility—a special responsibility to you who have stood with me in struggle. But sometimes I have to admit when I'm off by myself and I reflect on everything that has happened over the last two years, I really wonder whether or not I will be able to meet the role which history has cut out for me, which you have cut out for me, but I promise I am going to try. That, I promise … *[applause]*

My life, and the lives of my family, my mother, my comrades, my friends, has really been drastically transformed over the last two years. For what happened was that as our movement—and particularly our movement right here in Los Angeles, our movement to free political prisoners, our movement to free all oppressed people—as that movement began to grow and become stronger and develop in breadth, it just so happened that I was the one who—one of the ones who was singled out by the government's finger of repression. It just so happened that I was destined to become yet another symbol of what the government intends to do—what the government in this state would do to every person who refuses to be its passive, submissive subjects. *[applause]*

… And on the contrary, people let it be known that they would not be manipulated by terror. They would stand behind all their sisters and brothers who had been caught in the government's web of repression. I was one of those who was entrapped in that web. And the thousands and millions of people throughout the world came together in struggle and saved me from the fate the government had planned as an example to all of you who were disposed to resist. You intervened and saved my life, and now I am back among you, and as I was wrested away from you in struggle, so likewise I return in struggle. *[applause]* I return in

From American Radio Works, *Say It Plain, Say It Loud: A Century of Great African American Speeches*, http://americanradioworks. publicradio.org/features/blackspeech/adavis.html

struggle with a very simple message, a very simple message: We've just begun our fight. *[applause]* We've just begun.

And while we celebrate the victory of my own acquittal, and also of the release on appeal of a very beautiful brother from a Texas prison. I don't know if you know him, his name is Leotis Johnson. *[applause]* He was a SNCC, SCLC organizer in Texas and was framed up on a marijuana charge. He was released just a few days ago after having spent four years, four years in a Texas prison. *[applause]* We have to celebrate that victory, too, but as we celebrate these victories, we must also be about the business of transforming our joy, our enthusiasm into an even deeper commitment to all our sisters and brothers who do not yet have cause to celebrate.

And as I say this, I remember very, very vividly the hundreds of women who were with me in the New York Women's House of Detention, most of them black and brown women, all of them from the poorest strata of this society. I remember the women in the sterile cells of Marin County Jail, and the women in the dimly lit, windowless cells in Santa Clara County. There is still the savage inhumanity of Soledad Prison. One Soledad brother, our brother George, has been murdered. The two who survived were recently acquitted, but hundreds more are awaiting our aid and solidarity.

There are hundreds and thousands of Soledad Brothers, or San Quentin Brothers, or Folsom Brothers, of CIW sisters, all of whom are prisoners of an insanely criminal social order. So let us celebrate, but let us celebrate in the only way that is compatible with all the pain and suffering that so many of our sisters and brothers must face each morning as they awake to the oppressive sight of impenetrable concrete and steel. As they awake to the harsh banging of heavy iron doors opening and closing at the push of a button. As they awake each morning to the inevitable jangling of the keepers' keys—keys which are a constant reminder that freedom is so near, yet so far away. Millenniums and millenniums away.

So let us celebrate in the only way that is fitting. Let the joy of victory be the foundation of an undying vow; a renewed commitment to the cause of freedom. For we know now that victories are possible, though

the struggles they demand are long and arduous. So let our elation merge with a pledge to carry on this fight until a time when all the antiquated ugliness and brutality of jails and prisons linger on only as a mere, a mere memory of a nightmare ...

It has been said many times that one can learn a great deal about a society by looking towards its prisons. Look towards its dungeons and there you will see in concentrated and microcosmic form the sickness of the entire system. And today in the United States of America in 1972 there is something that is particularly revealing about the analogy between the prison and the larger society of which it is a reflection. For in a painfully real sense we are all prisoners of a society whose bombastic proclamations of freedom and justice for all are nothing but meaningless rhetoric.

For this society's accumulated wealth, its scientific achievements are swallowed up by the avarice of a few capitalists and by insane projects of war and other irrational ventures. We are imprisoned in a society where there is so much wealth and so many sophisticated scientific and technological skills that anyone with just a little bit of common sense can see the insanity of a continued existence of ghettos and barrios and the poverty which is there ... *[applause]*

... As black people, as brown people, as people of color, as working men and women in general, we know and we experience the agony of the struggle for existence each day. We are locked into that struggle. The parallels between our lives and the lives of our sisters and brothers behind bars are very clear. Yet there is a terrifying difference in degree between life on this side of the bars and life on the other side. And just as we must learn from the similarities and acquire an awareness of all the forces which oppress us out here, it is equally important that we understand that the plight of the prisoner unfolds in the rock-bottom realms of human existence ...

... The terror of life in prison, its awesome presence in the society at large, could not be disturbed.... For prisons are political weapons; they function as means of containing elements in this society which threaten the stability of the larger system.

In prisons, people who are actually or potentially disruptive of the status quo are confined, contained, punished, and in some cases, forced to undergo psychological treatment by mind-altering drugs.... The prison system is a weapon of repression. The government views young black and brown people as actually and potentially the most rebellious elements of this society. And thus the jails and prisons of this society are overflowing with young people of color. Anyone who has seen the streets of ghettos and barrios can already understand how easily a sister or a brother can fall victim to the police who are always there en masse.

Depending on the area, this country's prison population contains from 45 percent to 85 percent people of color. Nationally, 60 percent of all women prisoners are black. And tens of thousands of prisoners in city and county jails have never been convicted of any crime; they're simply there, victims—they're there under the control of insensitive, incompetent, and often blatantly racist public defenders who insist that they plead guilty even though they know that their client is just as innocent as they are. And for those who have committed a crime, we have to seek out the root cause. And we seek this cause not in them as individuals, but in the capitalist system that produces the need for crime in the first place. *[applause]*

As one student of the prisons system has said, "Thus the materially hungry must steal to survive, and the spiritually hungry commit anti-social acts because their human needs cannot be met in a property-oriented state. It is a fair estimate," he goes on to say, "that somewhere around 90 percent of the crimes committed would not be considered crimes or would not occur in a people-oriented society ..."

We must be about the business of building a movement so strong and so powerful that it will not only free individuals like me ... but one which will begin to attack the very foundations of the prison system itself. *[applause]*

And in doing this, the prison movement must be integrated into our struggles for black and brown liberation, and to our struggles for an end to material want and need. A very long struggle awaits us. And we know that it would be very romantic and idealistic to entertain immediate goals of tearing down all the walls of all the jails and prisons throughout this country. We should take on the task of freeing as many of

our sisters and brothers as possible. And at the same time we must demand the ultimate abolition of the prison system along with the revolutionary transformation of this society. *[applause]* However, however, within the context of fighting for fundamental changes, there is something else we must do.

We must try to alter the very fabric of life behind walls as much as is possible through struggle, and there are a thousand concrete issues around which we can build this movement: uncensored and unlimited mail privileges, visits of the prisoners' choice, minimum wage levels in prison, adequate medical care—and for women this is particularly important when you consider that in some prisons a woman, a pregnant woman has to fight just to get one glass of milk per day. I saw this in New York. There are other issues. Literature must be uncensored. Prisoners must have the right to school themselves as they see fit. If they wish to learn about Marxism, Leninism, and about socialist revolution, then they should have the right to do it ... *[applause]*

This is their right and they should have the full flexibility to do so. There should be no more "kangaroo courts" behind prison walls. *[applause]* There should be no more kangaroo courts wherein one can be charged with a simple violation of prison regulations and end up spending the rest of one's life there simply because the parole board would have it that way. *[applause]* And there must be an end, there must be an end to the tormenting, indeterminate sentence policy with which a prisoner like George Jackson could be sentenced from one year to life after having been convicted of stealing a mere $75. *[applause]*

For if you talk to any prisoner in the state of California and in other states where the indeterminate sentence law prevails, they will inevitably say that this is the most grueling aspect of life in prison. Going before a board of ex-cops, ex-narcotics agents, ex-FBI agents, and ex-prison guards and year after year after year after year being told to wait it out until next time.

These are just a few of the issues that we are going to have to deal with. And all of them, every single one of them, is the kind of issue which any decent human being should be able to understand.

The need, the very urgent need to join our sisters and brothers behind bars in their struggle was brought home during the rebellion and the massacre at Attica last year.

And I would like to close by reading a brief passage from a set of reflections I wrote in Marin County Jail upon hearing of the Attica revolt and massacre.

"The damage has been done, scores of men—some yet nameless—are dead. Unknown numbers are wounded ...

"But Attica was different from these other episodes in one very important respect. For this time the authorities were indicted by the very events themselves; they were caught red-handed in their lies. They were publicly exposed when to justify that massacre—a massacre which was led by Governor Rockefeller and agreed to by President Nixon—when they hastened to falsify what had occurred.

"Perhaps this in itself has pulled greater numbers of people from their socially-inflicted slumber. Many have already expressed outrage, but outrage is not enough. Governments and prison bureaucracies must be subjected to fears and unqualified criticism for their harsh and murderous repression. But even this is not enough, for this is not yet the root of the matter. People must take a forthright stand in active support of prisoners and their grievances. They must try to comprehend the eminently human content of prisoners' stirrings and struggles. For it is justice that we seek, and many of us can already envision a world unblemished by poverty and alienation, one where the prison would be but a vague memory, a relic of the past.

"But we also have immediate demands for justice right now, for fairness, and for room to think and live and act."

Thank you.

DRAWING CONCLUSIONS:

1. Consider how Dr. Davis's speech prophetically predicts the very struggles that shaped Black Liberation protests in 2020.

2. What features of the criminal legal system still resonate today, nearly fifty years after Dr. Davis's speech?

3.15 GRANDMASTER FLASH & THE FURIOUS FIVE, "THE MESSAGE," 1982

After the 1979 release of "Rapper's Delight," hip hop music skyrocketed to national and international prominence. Coupled with breakdancing, DJ-ing, and graffiti art, hip hop emerged as a cultural movement that voiced the frustrations and highlighted the artistic genius of urban youth. To fans and critics, "The Message" ranks as the most influential hip hop song of all time in its exploration of the challenges of urban living. "The Message" also reflects the continuation of artists offering stinging social commentary of America's racial inequities.

GUIDING QUESTIONS:

1. What picture is painted of urban living in the 1980s?
2. Why is "the jungle" used as the metaphor for urban spaces?
3. Why is this art form seemingly more brash than other literary explorations of the Black experience?

It's like a jungle sometimes
It makes me wonder how I keep from goin' under

Broken glass everywhere
People pissin' on the stairs, you know they just
    don't care
I can't take the smell, can't take the noise
Got no money to move out, I guess I got no
    choice
Rats in the front room, roaches in the back
Junkies in the alley with a baseball bat
I tried to get away but I couldn't get far
'Cause a man with a tow truck repossessed my car

Don't push me 'cause I'm close to the edge
I'm trying not to lose my head
It's like a jungle sometimes
It makes me wonder how I keep from goin' under

Standin' on the front stoop hangin' out the window
Watchin' all the cars go by, roarin' as the breezes
    blow
Crazy lady, livin' in a bag
Eatin' outta garbage pails, used to be a fag hag

Said she'll dance the tango, skip the light
    fandango
A Zircon princess seemed to lost her senses
Down at the peep show watchin' all the creeps
So she can tell her stories to the girls back home
She went to the city and got so so seditty
She had to get a pimp, she couldn't make it on
    her own

Don't push me cause I'm close to the edge
I'm trying not to lose my head
It's like a jungle sometimes
It makes me wonder how I keep from goin' under

It's like a jungle sometimes
It makes me wonder how I keep from goin' under

My brother's doin' bad, stole my mother's TV
Says she watches too much, it's just not healthy
All My Children in the daytime, Dallas at night
Can't even see the game or the Sugar Ray fight
The bill collectors, they ring my phone
And scare my wife when I'm not home
Got a bum education, double-digit inflation

From Grandmaster Flash & the Furious Five, "The Message," 1982.

Can't take the train to the job, there's a strike at
   the station
Neon King Kong standin' on my back
Can't stop to turn around, broke my sacroiliac
A mid-range migraine, cancered membrane
Sometimes I think I'm goin' insane
I swear I might hijack a plane!

Don't push me 'cause I'm close to the edge
I'm trying not to lose my head
It's like a jungle sometimes
It makes me wonder how I keep from goin' under

It's like a jungle sometimes
It makes me wonder how I keep from goin' under

A child is born with no state of mind
Blind to the ways of mankind
God is smilin' on you but he's frownin' too
Because only God knows what you'll go through
You'll grow in the ghetto livin' second-rate
And your eyes will sing a song called deep hate
The places you play and where you stay
Looks like one great big alleyway
You'll admire all the number-book takers
Thugs, pimps and pushers and the big
   money-makers
Drivin' big cars, spendin' twenties and tens
And you'll wanna grow up to be just like them,
   huh
Smugglers, scramblers, burglars, gamblers
Pickpocket peddlers, even panhandlers

You say I'm cool, huh, I'm no fool
But then you wind up droppin' outta high school
Now you're unemployed, all non-void
Walkin' round like you're Pretty Boy Floyd
Turned stick-up kid, but look what you done did
Got sent up for a eight-year bid
Now your manhood is took and you're a Maytag
Spend the next two years as a undercover fag
Bein' used and abused to serve like hell
'Til one day, you was found hung dead in the cell
It was plain to see that your life was lost
You was cold and your body swung back and
   forth
But now your eyes sing the sad, sad song
Of how you lived so fast and died so young so

Don't push me 'cause I'm close to the edge
I'm trying not to lose my head
It's like a jungle sometimes
It makes me wonder how I keep from goin' under

It's like a jungle sometimes
It makes me wonder how I keep from goin' under

DRAWING CONCLUSIONS:

1. Why is this considered the most influential song in hip hop history?
2. What does this song teach us about the shortcomings of the Modern Civil Rights Movement?
3. How does this song help explain why hip hop music and culture became a global juggernaut?

MODERN CIVIL RIGHTS LAWS AND POLICIES

4.1   EXECUTIVE ORDER 8802, 1941

President Franklin D. Roosevelt signed Executive Order 8802 in response to a threatened March on Washington by civil rights activists, most notably labor leader A. Phillip Randolph. The March on Washington Movement demanded an end to race-based employment discrimination in war-time industries. This effort was especially important for the increasing number of African Americans who had migrated to urban spaces in search for decent jobs as they fled the exploitative practices of the agricultural industry of the Jim Crow South.

GUIDING QUESTIONS:

1. What are the purposes of Executive Order 8802?
2. Why was an executive order the policy approach instead of Congressional legislation?
3. How will this executive order be enforced?
4. What does this document, and the threatened March on Washington, teach us about civil rights protest strategies—and pending outcomes—across decades and generations?

REAFFIRMING POLICY OF FULL PARTICIPATION IN THE DEFENSE PROGRAM BY ALL PERSONS, REGARDLESS OF RACE, CREED, COLOR, OR NATIONAL ORIGIN, AND DIRECTING CERTAIN ACTION IN FURTHERANCE OF SAID POLICY

June 25, 1941

Whereas it is the policy of the United States to encourage full participation in the national defense program by all citizens of the United States, regardless of race, creed, color, or national origin, in the firm belief that the democratic way of life within the Nation can be defended successfully only with the help and support of all groups within its borders; and

Whereas there is evidence that available and needed workers have been barred from employment in industries engaged in defense production solely because of considerations of race, creed, color, or national origin, to the detriment of workers' morale and of national unity:

Now, therefore, by virtue of the authority vested in me by the Constitution and the statutes, and as a prerequisite to the successful conduct of our national defense production effort, I do hereby reaffirm the policy of the United States that there shall be no discrimination in the employment of workers in defense industries or government because of race, creed, color, or national origin, and I do hereby declare that it is the duty of employers and of labor organizations, in furtherance of said policy and of this order, to provide for the full and equitable participation of all workers in defense industries, without discrimination because of race, creed, color, or national origin;

And it is hereby ordered as follows:

1. All departments and agencies of the Government of the United States concerned with vocational and training programs for defense production shall take special measures appropriate to assure that such programs are administered without discrimination because of race, creed, color, or national origin;
2. All contracting agencies of the Government of the United States shall include in all defense contracts hereafter negotiated by them a provision

From Executive Order 8802: Prohibition of Discrimination in the Defense Industries (1941), https://www.ourdocuments.gov/doc.php?flash=false&doc=72

obligating the contractor not to discriminate against any worker because of race, creed, color, or national origin;

3. There is established in the Office of Production Management a Committee on Fair Employment Practice, which shall consist of a chairman and four other members to be appointed by the President. The Chairman and members of the Committee shall serve as such without compensation but shall be entitled to actual and necessary transportation, subsistence and other expenses incidental to performance of their duties. The Committee shall receive and investigate complaints of discrimination in violation of the provisions of this order and shall take appropriate steps to redress grievances which it finds to be valid. The Committee shall also recommend to the several departments and agencies of the Government of the United States and to the President all measures which may be deemed by it necessary or proper to effectuate the provisions of this order.

Franklin D. Roosevelt
The White House
June 25, 1941

DRAWING CONCLUSIONS:

1. Does this executive order provide the power needed to end employment discrimination?
2. What authority does the Committee on Fair Employment practice have to combat employment discrimination?
3. How could African Americans use this executive order to gain access to better jobs?

4.2 *SWEATT V. PAINTER ET AL.* 339 U.S. 629 (1950)

While *Brown v. Board of Education* (1954) dealt the most critical blow to segregated education and segregation more broadly, there were several Supreme Court opinions that laid the legal groundwork for *Brown*. In *Sweatt v. Painter*, the Supreme Court offers a ruling that cleared the road just four years earlier and sets vital precedent for the *Brown* decision.

GUIDING QUESTIONS:

1. Who were the lawyers for the petitioner/students seeking admission to the University of Texas Law School?
2. What requirements did the state have to meet under the separate-but-equal doctrine?

W. J. DURHAM AND *THURGOOD MARSHALL* **ARGUED THE CAUSE FOR PETITIONER. WITH THEM ON THE BRIEF WERE** *ROBERT L. CARTER, WILLIAM R. MING, JR., JAMES M. NABRIT* **AND** *FRANKLIN H. WILLIAMS*.

Price Daniel, Attorney General of Texas, and *Joe R. Greenhill*, First Assistant Attorney General, argued the cause for respondents. With them on the brief was *E. Jacobson*, Assistant Attorney General ...

MR. CHIEF JUSTICE VINSON delivered the opinion of the Court.

This case and *McLaurin v. Oklahoma State Regents* ... present different aspects of this general question: To what extent does the Equal Protection Clause of the Fourteenth Amendment limit the power of a state to distinguish between students of different races in professional and graduate education in a state university? Broader issues have been urged for our consideration, but we adhere to the principle of deciding constitutional questions only in the context of the particular case before the Court ...

In the instant case, petitioner filed an application for admission to the University of Texas Law School for the February, 1946 term. His application was rejected solely because he is a Negro. Petitioner ... At that time, there was no law school in Texas which admitted Negroes ...

The University of Texas Law School, from which petitioner was excluded, was staffed by a faculty of sixteen full-time and three part-time professors, some of whom are nationally recognized authorities in their field. Its student body numbered 850. The library contained over 65,000 volumes. Among the other facilities available to the students were a law review, moot court facilities, scholarship funds, and Order of the Coif affiliation. The school's alumni occupy the most distinguished positions in the private practice of the law and in the public life of the State. It may properly be considered one of the nation's ranking law schools.

The law school for Negroes which was to have opened in February, 1947, would have had no independent faculty or library. The teaching was to be carried on by four members of the University of Texas Law School faculty, who were to maintain their offices at the University of Texas while teaching at both institutions. Few of the 10,000 volumes ordered for the library had arrived; nor was there any full-time librarian. The school lacked accreditation.

Since the trial of this case, respondents report the opening of a law school at the Texas State University for Negroes. It is apparently on the road to full accreditation. It has a faculty of five full-time professors; a student body of 23; a library of some 16,500 volumes

From *Sweatt v. Painter et al.* 339 U.S. 629 (1950).

serviced by a full-time staff; a practice court and legal aid association; and one alumnus who has become a member of the Texas Bar.

Whether the University of Texas Law School is compared with the original or the new law school for Negroes, we cannot find substantial equality in the educational opportunities offered white and Negro law students by the State. In terms of number of the faculty, variety of courses and opportunity for specialization, size of the student body, scope of the library, availability of law review and similar activities, the University of Texas Law School is superior. What is more important, the University of Texas Law School possesses to a far greater degree those qualities which are incapable of objective measurement but which make for greatness in a law school. Such qualities, to name but a few, include reputation of the faculty, experience of the administration, position and influence of the alumni, standing in the community, traditions and prestige. It is difficult to believe that one who had a free choice between these law schools would consider the question close.

Moreover, although the law is a highly learned profession, we are well aware that it is an intensely practical one. The law school, the proving ground for legal learning and practice, cannot be effective in isolation from the individuals and institutions with which the law interacts. Few students and no one who has practiced law would choose to study in an academic vacuum, removed from the interplay of ideas and the exchange of views with which the law is concerned. The law school to which Texas is willing to admit petitioner excludes from its student body members of the racial groups which number 85% of the population of the State and include most of the lawyers, witnesses, jurors, judges and other officials with whom petitioner will inevitably be dealing when he becomes a member of the Texas Bar. With such a substantial and significant segment of society excluded, we cannot conclude that the education offered petitioner is substantially equal to that which he would receive if admitted to the University of Texas Law School.

It may be argued that excluding petitioner from that school is no different from excluding white students from the new law school. This contention overlooks realities. It is unlikely that a member of a group so decisively in the majority, attending a school with rich traditions and prestige which only a history of consistently maintained excellence could command, would claim that the opportunities afforded him for legal education were unequal to those held open to petitioner. That such a claim, if made, would be dishonored by the State, is no answer. "Equal protection of the laws is not achieved through indiscriminate imposition of inequalities." *Shelley* v. *Kraemer*, 334 U. S. 1, 22 (1948).

It is fundamental that these cases concern rights which are personal and present. This Court has stated unanimously that "The State must provide [legal education] for [petitioner] in conformity with the equal protection clause of the Fourteenth Amendment and provide it as soon as it does for applicants of any other group." *Sipuel v. Board of Regents*, 332 U. S. 631, 633 (1948). That case "did not present the issue whether a state might not satisfy the equal protection clause of the Fourteenth Amendment by establishing a separate law school for Negroes." *Fisher v. Hurst*, 333 U. S. 147, 150 (1948). In *Missouri ex rel. Gaines* v. *Canada*, 305 U. S. 337, 351 (1938), the Court, speaking through Chief Justice Hughes, declared that "petitioner's right was a personal one. It was as an individual that he was entitled to the equal protection of the laws, and the State was bound to furnish him within its borders facilities for legal education substantially equal to those which the State there afforded for persons of the white race, whether or not other negroes sought the same opportunity." These are the only cases in this Court which present the issue of the constitutional validity of race distinctions in state-supported graduate and professional education.

In accordance with these cases, petitioner may claim his full constitutional right: legal education equivalent to that offered by the State to students of other races. Such education is not available to him in a separate law school as offered by the State. We cannot, therefore, agree with respondents that the doctrine of *Plessy v. Ferguson*, 163 U. S. 537 (1896), requires affirmance of the judgment below. Nor need we reach petitioner's contention that *Plessy v. Ferguson* should be reexamined in the light of contemporary knowledge respecting the purposes of the Fourteenth Amendment and the effects of racial segregation. See *supra*, p. 631.

We hold that the Equal Protection Clause of the Fourteenth Amendment requires that petitioner be admitted to the University of Texas Law School. The judgment is reversed and the cause is remanded for proceedings not inconsistent with this opinion.

Reversed.

DRAWING CONCLUSIONS:

1. Why did the NAACP legal team first attempt to desegregate college-level, professional schools instead of primary-level schools?
2. What does the Supreme Court state about equal facilities in this case?
3. What rulings and cases does the Court rely on to reach this determination?

4.3 EXECUTIVE ORDER 10925—ESTABLISHING THE PRESIDENT'S COMMITTEE ON EQUAL EMPLOYMENT OPPORTUNITY, 1961 (EXCERPTS)

Executive Order 10925 created the President's Committee on Equal Employment Opportunity. It required government contractors "take affirmative action..." to ensure that applicants and employees are treated "...without regard to their race..." This and subsequent executive orders, along with congressional legislation, emerged in response to demands for employment equality.

GUIDING QUESTIONS:

1. What are the purposes of Executive Order 10925?
2. Why was an executive order the policy approach instead of Congressional legislation?
3. How will this executive order be enforced to ensure employment equality?

March 6, 1961

Whereas discrimination because of race, creed, color, or national origin is contrary to the Constitutional principles and policies of the United States; and 13 CFR 1960 Supp.

Whereas it is the plain and positive obligation of the United States Government to promote and ensure equal opportunity for all qualified persons, without regard to race, creed, color, or national origin, employed or seeking employment with the Federal Government and on government contracts; and

Whereas it is the policy of the executive branch of the Government to encourage by positive measures equal opportunity for all qualified persons within the Government; and

Whereas it is in the general interest and welfare of the United States to promote its economy, security, and national defense through the most efficient and effective utilization of all available manpower; and

Whereas a review and analysis of existing Executive orders, practices, and government agency procedures relating to government employment and compliance with existing non-discrimination contract provisions reveal an urgent need for expansion and strengthening of efforts to promote full equality of employment opportunity; and

Whereas a single governmental committee should be charged with responsibility for accomplishing these objectives:

Now, therefore, by virtue of the authority vested in me as President of the United States by the Constitution and statutes of the United States, it is ordered as follows:

PART I—ESTABLISHMENT OF THE PRESIDENT'S COMMITTEE ON EQUAL EMPLOYMENT OPPORTUNITY

SECTION 101. There is hereby established the President's Committee on Equal Employment Opportunity.

PART II—NONDISCRIMINATION IN GOVERNMENT EMPLOYMENT

SECTION 201. The President's Committee on Equal Employment Opportunity established by this order

From The American Presidency Project, UC–Santa Barbara, https://www.presidency.ucsb.edu/documents/executive-order-10925-establishing-the-presidents-committee-equal-employment-opportunity is directed immediately to scrutinize and study employment practices of the Government of the United States, and to consider and recommend additional affirmative steps which should be taken by executive departments and agencies to realize more fully the national policy of nondiscrimination within the executive branch of the Government.

SEC. 202. All executive departments and agencies are directed to initiate forthwith studies of current government employment practices within their responsibility. The studies shall be in such form as the Committee may prescribe and shall include statistics on current employment patterns, a review of current procedures, and the recommendation of positive measures for the elimination of any discrimination, direct or indirect, which now exists. Reports and recommendations shall be submitted to the Executive Vice Chairman of the Committee no later than sixty days from the effective date of this order, and the Committee, after considering such reports and recommendations, shall report to the President on the current situation and recommend positive measures to accomplish the objectives of this order ...

PART III—OBLIGATIONS OF GOVERNMENT CONTRACTORS AND SUBCONTRACTORS

SUBPART A—CONTRACTORS' AGREEMENTS

SECTION 301. Except in contracts exempted in accordance with section 303 of this order, all government contracting agencies shall include in every government contract hereafter entered into the following provisions:

"In connection with the performance of work under this contract, the contractor agrees as follows:

"(1) The contractor will not discriminate against any employee or applicant for employment because of race, creed, color, or national origin. The contractor will take affirmative action to ensure that applicants are employed, and that employees are treated during employment, without regard to their race, creed, color, or national origin. Such action shall include, but not be limited to, the following: employment, upgrading, demotion or transfer; recruitment or

recruitment advertising; layoff or termination; rates of pay or other forms of compensation; and selection for training, including apprenticeship. The contractor agrees to post in conspicuous places, available to employees and applicants for employment, notices to be provided by the contracting officer setting forth the provisions of this nondiscrimination clause.

"(2) The contractor will, in all solicitations or advertisements for employees placed by or on behalf of the contractor, state that all qualified applicants will receive consideration for employment without regard to race, creed, color, or national origin ...

SUBPART B—LABOR UNIONS AND REPRESENTATIVES OF WORKERS

SEC. 304. The Committee shall use its best efforts, directly and through contracting agencies, contractors, state and local officials and public and private agencies, and all other available instrumentalities, to cause any labor union, recruiting agency or other representative of workers who is or may be engaged in work under Government contracts to cooperate with, and to comply in the implementation of, the purposes of this order ...

SUBPART C—POWERS AND DUTIES OF THE PRESIDENTS COMMITTEE ON EQUAL EMPLOYMENT OPPORTUNITY AND OF CONTRACTING AGENCIES

SEC. 306. The Committee shall adopt such rules and regulations and issue such orders as it deems necessary and appropriate to achieve the purposes of this order, including the purposes of Part II hereof relating to discrimination in Government employment ...

SEC. 309. (a) The Committee may itself investigate the employment practices of any Government contractor or subcontractor, or initiate such investigation by the appropriate contracting agency or through the Secretary of Labor, to determine whether or not the contractual provisions specified in section 301 of this order have been violated.

SUBPART D—SANCTIONS AND PENALTIES

SEC. 312. In accordance with such rules, regulations or orders as the Committee may issue or adopt, the Committee or the appropriate contracting agency may:

(a) Publish, or cause to be published, the names of contractors or unions which it has concluded have complied or have failed to comply with the provisions of this order or of the rules, regulations, and orders of the Committee.

(b) Recommend to the Department of Justice that, in cases where there is substantial or material violation or the threat of substantial or material violation of the contractual provisions set forth in section 301 of this order, appropriate proceedings be brought to enforce those provisions, including the enjoining, within the limitations of applicable law, of organizations, individuals or groups who prevent directly or indirectly, or seek to prevent directly or indirectly, compliance with the aforesaid provisions.

(c) Recommend to the Department of Justice that criminal proceedings be brought for the furnishing of false information to any contracting agency or to the Committee as the case may be ...

John F. Kennedy
The White House
March 6, 1961

DRAWING CONCLUSIONS:

1. Why is this executive order directed at government contractors? Which institutions have government contracts of some kind?

2. Why does this executive order require the creation of studies and reports about employment discrimination?

3. What is the "affirmative action" government contractors are required to take to ensure employment equality?

4. What "sanctions and penalties" can the Committee on Equal Employment Opportunity levy against noncompliant contractors?

4.4 CIVIL RIGHTS ACT OF 1964 (EXCERPTS)

The Civil Rights Act of 1964 was a sweeping, broad legislation that brought a formal end to the system of legal segregation. The following excerpts from this historic bill highlight the ways Congress sought to address the various components of Jim Crow.

GUIDING QUESTIONS:

1. Did Congress intend for the Civil Rights Act of 1964 to end segregation? If so, how?
2. What areas of discrimination does Congress address within this bill?

AN ACT

To enforce the constitutional right to vote, to confer jurisdiction upon the district courts of the United States to provide injunctive relief against discrimination in public accommodations, to authorize the Attorney General to institute suits to protect constitutional rights in public facilities and public education, to extend the Commission on Civil Rights, to prevent discrimination in federally assisted programs, to establish a Commission on Equal Employment Opportunity, and for other purposes.

Be it enacted by the Senate and House of Representatives of the United States of America in Congress assembled, That this Act may be cited as the "Civil Rights Act of 1964."

TITLE I—VOTING RIGHTS

SEC. 101.

"(2) No person acting under color of law shall—

"(A) in determining whether any individual is qualified under State law or laws to vote in any Federal election, apply any standard, practice, or procedure different from the standards, practices, or procedures applied under such law or laws to other individuals within the same county, parish, or similar political subdivision who have been found by State officials to be qualified to vote;

"(B) deny the right of any individual to vote in any Federal election because of an error or omission on any record or paper relating to any application, registration, or other act requisite to voting, if such error or omission is not material in determining whether such individual is qualified under State law to vote in such election; or

"(C) employ any literacy test as a qualification for voting in any Federal election unless (i) such test is administered to each individual and is conducted wholly in writing, and (ii) a certified copy of the test and of the answers given by the individual is furnished to him within twenty-five days of the submission of his request ...

TITLE II—INJUNCTIVE RELIEF AGAINST DISCRIMINATION IN PLACES OF PUBLIC ACCOMMODATION

SEC. 201. (a) All persons shall be entitled to the full and equal enjoyment of the goods, services, facilities, and privileges, advantages, and accommodations of any place of public accommodation, as defined in this section, without discrimination or segregation on the ground of race, color, religion, or national origin.

(b) Each of the following establishments which serves the public is a place of public accommodation within the meaning of this title if its operations affect commerce, or if discrimination or segregation by it is supported by State action:

From Civil Rights Act (1964), https://www.ourdocuments.gov/doc.php?flash=false&doc=97

(1) any inn, hotel, motel, or other establishment which provides lodging to transient guests ...
(2) any restaurant, cafeteria, lunchroom, lunch counter, soda fountain, or other facility principally engaged in selling food for consumption on the premises ...
(3) any motion picture house, theater, concert hall, sports arena, stadium or other place of exhibition or entertainment ...

SEC. 202. All persons shall be entitled to be free, at any establishment or place, from discrimination or segregation of any kind on the ground of race, color, religion, or national origin, if such discrimination or segregation is or purports to be required by any law, statute, ordinance, regulation, rule, or order of a State or any agency or political subdivision thereof.

SEC. 203. No person shall (a) withhold, deny, or attempt to withhold or deny, or deprive or attempt to deprive, any person of any right or privilege secured by section 201 or 202, or (b) intimidate, threaten, or coerce, or attempt to intimidate, threaten, or coerce any person with the purpose of interfering with any right or privilege secured by section 201 or 202, or (c) punish or attempt to punish any person for exercising or attempting to exercise any right or privilege secured by section 201 or 202.

SEC. 204. (a) Whenever any person has engaged or there are reasonable grounds to believe that any person is about to engage in any act or practice prohibited by section 203, a civil action for preventive relief ...

SEC. 206. (a) Whenever the Attorney General has reasonable cause to believe that any person or group of persons is engaged in a pattern or practice of resistance to the full enjoyment of any of the rights secured by this title, and that the pattern or practice is of such a nature and is intended to deny the full exercise of the rights herein described, the Attorney General may bring a civil action in the appropriate district court of the United States ...

TITLE III—DESEGREGATION OF PUBLIC FACILITIES

SEC. 301. (a) Whenever the Attorney General receives a complaint in writing signed by an individual to the effect that he is being deprived of or threatened with the loss of his right to the equal protection of the laws, on account of his race, color, religion, or national origin, by being denied equal utilization of any public facility which is owned, operated, or managed by or on behalf of any State or subdivision thereof, other than a public school or public college as defined in section 401 of title IV hereof, and the Attorney General believes the complaint is meritorious ... the Attorney General is authorized to institute for or in the name of the United States a civil action in any appropriate district court of the United States against such parties and for such relief as may be appropriate ...

TITLE IV—DESEGREGATION OF PUBLIC EDUCATION SUITS BY THE ATTORNEY GENERAL

SEC. 407. (a) Whenever the Attorney General receives a complaint in writing—

(1) signed by a parent or group of parents to the effect that his or their minor children, as members of a class of persons similarly situated, are being deprived by a school board of the equal protection of the laws, or
(2) signed by an individual, or his parent, to the effect that he has been denied admission to or not permitted to continue in attendance at a public college by reason of race, color, religion, or national origin, and the Attorney General believes the complaint is meritorious ... the Attorney General is authorized ... to institute for or in the name of the United States a civil action in any appropriate district court of the United States against such parties and for such relief as may be appropriate ...

TITLE V—COMMISSION ON CIVIL RIGHTS "DUTIES OF THE COMMISSION"

SEC. 104. (a) The Commission shall—

"(1) investigate allegations in writing under oath or affirmation that certain citizens of the United States are being deprived of their right to vote and have that vote counted by reason of their color, race, religion, or national origin; which writing, under oath or affirmation, shall set forth the facts upon which such belief or beliefs are based;

"(2) study and collect information concerning legal developments constituting a denial of equal protection of the laws under the Constitution because of race, color, religion or national origin or in the administration of justice;

"(3) appraise the laws and policies of the Federal Government with respect to denials of equal protection of the laws under the Constitution because of race, color, religion or national origin or in the administration of justice;

"(4) serve as a national clearinghouse for information in respect to denials of equal protection of the laws because of race, color, religion or national origin, including but not limited to the fields of voting, education, housing, employment, the use of public facilities, and transportation, or in the administration of justice;

"(5) investigate allegations, made in writing and under oath or affirmation, that citizens of the United States are unlawfully being accorded or denied the right to vote, or to have their votes properly counted, in any election of presidential electors, Members of the United States Senate, or of the House of Representatives, as a result of any patterns or practice of fraud or discrimination in the conduct of such election; and ..."

TITLE VI—NONDISCRIMINATION IN FEDERALLY ASSISTED PROGRAMS

SEC. 601. No person in the United States shall, on the ground of race, color, or national origin, be excluded from participation in, be denied the benefits of, or be subjected to discrimination under any program or activity receiving Federal financial assistance.

SEC. 602. Each Federal department and agency which is empowered to extend Federal financial assistance to any program or activity, by way of grant, loan, or contract other than a contract of insurance or guaranty, is authorized and directed to effectuate the provisions of section 601 with respect to such program or activity by issuing rules, regulations, or orders of general applicability which shall be consistent with achievement of the objectives of the statute authorizing the financial assistance in connection with which the action is taken ...

TITLE VII—EQUAL EMPLOYMENT OPPORTUNITY DISCRIMINATION BECAUSE OF RACE, COLOR, RELIGION, SEX, OR NATIONAL ORIGIN

SEC. 703. (a) It shall be an unlawful employment practice for an employer—

(1) to fail or refuse to hire or to discharge any individual, or otherwise to discriminate against any individual with respect to his compensation, terms, conditions, or privileges of employment, because of such individual's race, color, religion, sex, or national origin; or

(2) to limit, segregate, or classify his employees in any way which would deprive or tend to deprive any individual of employment opportunities or otherwise adversely affect his status as an employee, because of such individual's race, color, religion, sex, or national origin.

(b) It shall be an unlawful employment practice for an employment agency to fail or refuse to refer for employment, or otherwise to discriminate against, any individual because of his race, color, religion, sex, or national origin, or to classify or refer for employment any individual on the basis of his race, color, religion, sex, or national origin.

(c) It shall be an unlawful employment practice for a labor organization—

(1) to exclude or to expel from its membership, or otherwise to discriminate against, any individual because of his race, color, religion, sex, or national origin;

(2) to limit, segregate, or classify its membership, or to classify or fail or refuse to refer for employment any individual, in any way which would deprive or tend to deprive any individual of employment opportunities, or would limit such

employment opportunities or otherwise adversely affect his status as an employee or as an applicant for employment, because of such individual's race, color, religion, sex, or national origin; or

(3) to cause or attempt to cause an employer to discriminate against an individual in violation of this section.

(d) It shall be an unlawful employment practice for any employer, labor organization, or joint labor-management committee controlling apprenticeship or other training or retraining, including on-the-job training programs to discriminate against any individual because of his race, color, religion, sex, or national origin in admission to, or employment in, any program established to provide apprenticeship or other training …

(j) Nothing contained in this title shall be interpreted to require any employer, employment agency, labor organization, or joint labor-management committee subject to this title to grant preferential treatment to any individual or to any group because of the race, color, religion, sex, or national origin of such individual or group on account of an imbalance which may exist with respect to the total number or percentage of persons of any race, color, religion, sex, or national origin employed by any employer, referred or classified for employment by any employment agency or labor organization …

EQUAL EMPLOYMENT OPPORTUNITY COMMISSION

SEC. 705. (a) There is hereby created a Commission to be known as the Equal Employment Opportunity Commission, which shall be composed of five members, not more than three of whom shall be members of the same political party, who shall be appointed by the President by and with the advice and consent of the Senate …

PREVENTION OF UNLAWFUL EMPLOYMENT PRACTICES

SEC. 706. (a) Whenever it is charged in writing under oath by a person claiming to be aggrieved, or a written charge has been filed by a member of the Commission where he has reasonable cause to believe a violation of this title has occurred … the Commission shall furnish such employer, employment agency, or labor organization (hereinafter referred to as the "respondent") with a copy of such charge and shall make an investigation of such charge …

(g) If the court finds that the respondent has intentionally engaged in or is intentionally engaging in an unlawful employment practice charged in the complaint, the court may enjoin the respondent from engaging in such unlawful employment practice, and order such affirmative action as may be appropriate, which may include reinstatement or hiring of employees, with or without back pay (payable by the employer, employment agency, or labor organization, as the case may be, responsible for the unlawful employment practice) …

SEC. 707. (a) Whenever the Attorney General has reasonable cause to believe that any person or group of persons is engaged in a pattern or practice of resistance to the full enjoyment of any of the rights secured by this title … the Attorney General may bring a civil action in the appropriate district court of the United States by filing with it a complaint …

Approved July 2, 1964.

DRAWING CONCLUSIONS:

1. What are the authorities granted to the Attorney General, Commission on Civil Rights, and the Equal Employment Opportunities Committee?
2. Are the provisions of the legislation strong enough to completely end segregation and race discrimination?

4.5 VOTING RIGHTS ACT OF 1965 (EXCERPTS) AND TWENTY-FOURTH AND TWENTY-SIXTH AMENDMENTS TO THE UNITED STATES CONSTITUTION

The Voting Rights Act of 1965 ushered in an era of political agency that African Americans had not witnessed since Reconstruction. As a result, African Americans across the country were voted into political leadership at the local, state, and federal levels. Coupled with the Civil Rights Act of 1964, it serves as a shining, statutory victory of the Modern Civil Rights Movement.

GUIDING QUESTIONS:

1. Why was the Voting Rights Act of 1965 necessary?
2. What realities and events during the protest era of the Modern Civil Rights Movement prompted Congress to pass this legislation?

An act to enforce the fifteenth amendment to the Constitution of the United States, and for other purposes.

Be it enacted by the Senate and House of Representatives of the United States of America in Congress assembled, That this Act shall be known as the "Voting Rights Act of 1965."

SEC. 2. No voting qualification or prerequisite to voting, or standard, practice, or procedure shall be imposed or applied by any State or political subdivision to deny or abridge the right of any citizen of the United States to vote on account of race or color ...

SEC. 4. (a) To assure that the right of citizens of the United States to vote is not denied or abridged on account of race or color, no citizen shall be denied the right to vote in any Federal, State, or local election because of his failure to comply with any test or device in any State with respect to which the determinations have been made under subsection (b) or in any political subdivision with respect to which such determinations have been made as a separate unit, unless the United States District Court for the District of Columbia in an action for a declaratory judgment brought by such State or subdivision against the United States has determined that no such test or device has been used during the five years preceding the filing of the action for the purpose or with the effect of denying or abridging the right to vote on account of race or color: Provided, That no such declaratory judgment shall issue with respect to any plaintiff for a period of five years after the entry of a final judgment of any court of the United States, other than the denial of a declaratory judgment under this section, whether entered prior to or after the enactment of this Act, determining that denials or abridgments of the right to vote on account of race or color through the use of such tests or devices have occurred anywhere in the territory of such plaintiff. An action pursuant to this subsection shall be heard and determined by a court of three judges in accordance with the provisions of section 2284 of title 28 of the United States Code and any appeal shall lie to the Supreme Court. The court shall retain jurisdiction of any action pursuant to this subsection for five years after judgment and shall reopen the action upon motion of the Attorney General alleging that a test or device has been used for the

From Voting Rights Act (1965), https://www.ourdocuments.gov/doc.php?flash=false&doc=100 and United States Constitution.

purpose or with the effect of denying or abridging the right to vote on account of race or color.

If the Attorney General determines that he has no reason to believe that any such test or device has been used during the five years preceding the filing of the action for the purpose or with the effect of denying or abridging the right to vote on account of race or color, he shall consent to the entry of such judgment.

(b) The provisions of subsection (a) shall apply in any State or in any political subdivision of a state which (1) the Attorney General determines maintained on November 1, 1964, any test or device, and with respect to which (2) the Director of the Census determines that less than 50 percentum of the persons of voting age residing therein were registered on November 1, 1964, or that less than 50 percentum of such persons voted in the presidential election of November 1964.

A determination or certification of the Attorney General or of the Director of the Census under this section or under section 6 or section 13 shall not be reviewable in any court and shall be effective upon publication in the Federal Register.

(c) The phrase "test or device" shall mean any requirement that a person as a prerequisite for voting or registration for voting (1) demonstrate the ability to read, write, understand, or interpret any matter, (2) demonstrate any educational achievement or his knowledge of any particular subject, (3) possess good moral character, or (4) prove his qualifications by the voucher of registered voters or members of any other class …

SEC. 5. Whenever a State or political subdivision with respect to which the prohibitions set forth in section 4(a) are in effect shall enact or seek to administer any voting qualification or prerequisite to voting, or standard, practice, or procedure with respect to voting different from that in force or effect on November 1, 1964, such State or subdivision may institute an action in the United States District Court for the District of Columbia for a declaratory judgment that such qualification, prerequisite, standard, practice, or procedure does not have the purpose and will not have the effect of denying or abridging

the right to vote on account of race or color, and unless and until the court enters such judgment no person shall be denied the right to vote for failure to comply with such qualification, prerequisite, standard, practice, or procedure: Provided, That such qualification, prerequisite, standard, practice, or procedure may be enforced without such proceeding if the qualification, prerequisite, standard, practice, or procedure has been submitted by the chief legal officer or other appropriate official of such State or subdivision to the Attorney General and the Attorney General has not interposed an objection within sixty days after such submission, except that neither the Attorney General's failure to object nor a declaratory judgment entered under this section shall bar a subsequent action to enjoin enforcement of such qualification, prerequisite, standard, practice, or procedure. Any action under this section shall be heard and determined by a court of three judges in accordance with the provisions of section 2284 of title 28 of the United States Code and any appeal shall lie to the Supreme Court …

SEC. 10. (a) The Congress finds that the requirement of the payment of a poll tax as a precondition to voting (i) precludes persons of limited means from voting or imposes unreasonable financial hardship upon such persons as a precondition to their exercise of the franchise, (ii) does not bear a reasonable relationship to any legitimate State interest in the conduct of election, and (iii) in some areas has the purpose or effect of denying persons the right to vote because of race or color. Upon the bases of these finding, Congress declares that the constitutional right of citizens to votes is denied or abridged in some areas by the requirement of the payment of a poll tax as a precondition to voting …

SEC. 11. (a) No person acting under color of law shall fail or refuse to permit any person to vote who is entitled to vote under any provision of this Act or is otherwise qualified to vote, or willfully fail or refuse to tabulate, count, and report such person's vote.

(b) No person, whether acting under color of law or otherwise, shall intimidate, threaten, or coerce, or attempt to intimidate, threaten, or coerce any person for voting or attempting to vote, or intimidate, threaten, or coerce, or attempt to intimidate, threaten, or coerce any person for urging or aiding any person to vote or attempt to vote, or intimidate, threaten, or coerce any person for exercising any powers or duties under section 3(a), 6, 8, 9, 10, or 12(e) ...

TWENTY-FOURTH AND TWENTY-SIXTH AMENDMENTS TO THE UNITED STATES CONSTITUTION

Amendment XXIV, January 23, 1964

1. The right of citizens of the United States to vote in any primary or other election for President or Vice President for electors for President or Vice President, or for Senator or Representative in Congress, shall not be denied or abridged by the United States or any State by reason of failure to pay any poll tax or other tax.

2. The Congress shall have power to enforce this article by appropriate legislation.

Amendment XXVI, July 1, 1971

1. The right of citizens of the United States, who are eighteen years of age or older, to vote shall not be denied or abridged by the United States or by any State on account of age.

2. The Congress shall have power to enforce this article by appropriate legislation.

DRAWING CONCLUSIONS:

1. Why were the Twenty-Fourth and Twenty-Sixth Amendments necessary to advance political participation on the part of African Americans and young adults?

2. What were the immediate and long-term outcomes of the Voting Rights Act of 1965 and the Twenty-Fourth and Twenty-Sixth Amendments?

4.6 BLACK OCCUPATIONAL SHARES, 1960S–2000S

While often overlooked due to the dramatic clashes around desegregating schools, voting rights, and public accommodations, equal employment opportunity was an issue central to the long-standing Black liberation movement(s). The graph shown here highlights occupational data since the 1960s, revealing important and intriguing trends associated with employment growth or the lack thereof.

GUIDING QUESTIONS:

1. What does this graph show regarding regional differences in occupational growth?
2. How do we account for these regional differences in occupational growth?

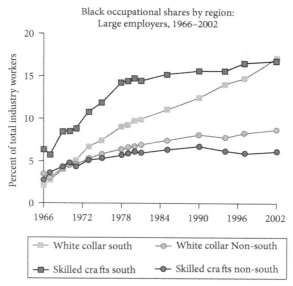

FIGURE 1 BLACK OCCUPATIONAL SHARES, 1960S-2000S

DRAWING CONCLUSIONS:

1. What does this chart teach us about the connections between employment opportunities and migratory trends?

2. Why is the occupational status of African Americas stagnant outside the South?

From *Equal Employment Opportunity Commission: Job Patterns for Minorities and Women in Private Industry*, various years (Gavin Wright, *Sharing the Prize* [Cambridge, MA: Harvard University Press], Kindle edition).

4.7 VIOLENT CRIME CONTROL AND LAW ENFORCEMENT ACT OF 1994

The Violent Crime Control and Law Enforcement Act, often referred to as the "Clinton Crime Bill," is widely considered the key policy that fueled the growth of mass incarceration in the United States. The bill provided billions of dollars to expand and militarize police departments across the country. The bill required extended prison sentencing through the now infamous "three strikes" rule. And the bill includes enhanced punitive approaches to a wide array of criminal activities. Excerpts and summaries are included here because the bill highlights the political response—policing and incarceration—to the socioeconomic challenges faced in urban America .

GUIDING QUESTIONS:

1. Why does this bill focus so heavily on policing and incarceration as solutions to crime?
2. Why is immigration control included in the bill?
3. What kinds of "preventive programs" will emerge from the "input of experienced police officers?"
4. What areas of the bill actually address public safety?

The Violent Crime Control and Law Enforcement Act of 1994 represents the bipartisan product of six years of hard work. It is the largest crime bill in the history of the country and will provide for 100,000 new police officers, $9.7 billion in funding for prisons and $6.1 billion in funding for prevention programs which were designed with significant input from experienced police officers. The Act also significantly expands the government's ability to deal with problems caused by criminal aliens. The Crime Bill provides $2.6 billion in additional funding for the FBI, DEA, INS, United States Attorneys, and other Justice Department components, as well as the Federal courts and the Treasury Department. Some of the most significant provisions of the bill are summarized below:

SUBSTANTIVE CRIMINAL PROVISIONS

ASSAULT WEAPONS

Bans the manufacture of 19 military-style assault weapons, assault weapons with specific combat features, "copy-cat" models, and certain high-capacity ammunition magazines of more than ten rounds.

DEATH PENALTY

Expands the Federal death penalty to cover about 60 offenses, including terrorist homicides, murder of a Federal law enforcement officer, large-scale drug trafficking, drive-by-shootings resulting in death and carjackings resulting in death.

DOMESTIC ABUSERS AND FIREARMS

Prohibits firearms sales to and possession by persons subject to family violence restraining orders.

FIREARMS LICENSING

Strengthens Federal licensing standards for firearms dealers.

FRAUD

Creates new insurance and telemarketing fraud categories. Expands Federal jurisdiction to cases that do not involve the use of delivery services to commit a

From U.S. Department of Justice Fact Sheet, https://www.ncjrs.gov/txtfiles/billfs.txt

fraud. Provides special sentencing enhancements for fraud crimes committed against the elderly.

GANG CRIMES
Provides new and stiffer penalties for violent and drug trafficking crimes committed by gang members.

IMMIGRATION
Provides for enhanced penalties for alien smuggling, illegal reentry after deportation and other immigration-related crimes. (See Part II).

JUVENILES
Authorizes adult prosecution of those 13 and older charged with certain serious violent crimes. Prohibits the sale or transfer of a firearm to or possession of certain firearms by juveniles. Triples the maximum penalties for using children to distribute drugs in or near a protected zone, i.e., schools, playgrounds, video arcades and youth centers.

REGISTRATION OF SEXUALLY VIOLENT OFFENDERS
Requires states to enact statutes or regulations which require those determined to be sexually violent predators or who are convicted of sexually violent offenses to register with appropriate state law enforcement agencies for ten years after release from prison. Requires state prison officials to notify appropriate agencies of the release of such individuals. Requires states to criminally punish those who fail to register. States which fail to establish registration systems may have Federal grant money reduced.

REPEAT SEX OFFENDERS
Doubles the maximum term of imprisonment for repeat sex offenders convicted of Federal sex crimes.

THREE STRIKES
Mandatory life imprisonment without possibility of parole for Federal offenders with three or more convictions for serious violent felonies or drug trafficking crimes.

VICTIMS OF CRIME
Allows victims of Federal violent and sex crimes to speak at the sentencing of their assailants.

Strengthens requirements for sex offenders and child molesters to pay restitution to their victims. Improves the Federal Crime Victims' Fund and the victim-related programs it supports.

OTHER
Creates new crimes or enhances penalties for: drive-by-shootings, use of semi-automatic weapons, sex offenses, crimes against the elderly, interstate firearms trafficking, firearms theft and smuggling, arson, hate crimes and interstate domestic violence.

IMMIGRATION INITIATIVES
The Crime Bill contains specialized enforcement provisions respecting immigration and criminal aliens. Those programs are highlighted here:

$1.2 billion for border control, criminal alien deportations, asylum reform and a criminal alien tracking center.

$1.8 billion to reimburse states for incarceration of illegal criminal aliens. (See State Criminal Alien Assistance Program (SCAAP) Grants in Section III).

Enhanced penalties for failure to depart the United States after a deportation order or reentry after deportation.

Expedited deportation for aliens who are not lawful permanent residents and who are convicted of aggravated felonies.

Statutory authority for abused spouses and spouses with abused children to petition for permanent residency or suspension of deportation.

GRANT PROGRAMS FOR 1995
Most of these programs are authorized for six years beginning October 1, 1994. Some are formula grants, awarded to states or localities based on population, crime rate or some other combination of factors. Many are competitive grants. All grants will require an application process and are administered by the Department of Justice unless otherwise noted. As always, all funds for the years 1996–2000 are subject to appropriation by the Congress.

BRADY IMPLEMENTATION
Competitive grant program for states to upgrade criminal history records keeping so as to permit

compliance with the Brady Act. $100 million appropriated in 1995. In addition, the Brady Act authorizes $100 million for FY 1996. $50 million of this amount is authorized to be expended from the Violent Crime Control Act Trust Fund.

BYRNE GRANTS

Formula grant program for states for use in more than 20 law enforcement purposes, including state and local drug task force efforts. $450 million appropriated for the formula grant program in 1995. $550 million authorized in 1996–2000 for both formula and discretionary.

COMMUNITY POLICING

Competitive grant program (COPS Program) to put 100,000 police officers on the streets in community policing programs. $1.3 billion available in 1995. $7.5 billion authorized in 1996–2000.

COMMUNITY SCHOOLS

Formula grant program administered by the Department of Health and Human Services for supervised afterschool, weekend, and summer programs for at-risk youth. $25.9 million available in 1995. $567 million authorized in 1995–2000.

CORRECTIONAL FACILITIES/BOOT CAMPS

Formula and competitive grant program for state corrections agencies to build and operate correctional facilities, including boot camps and other alternatives to incarceration, to insure that additional space will be available to put—and keep—violent offenders incarcerated. Fifty percent of money to be set aside for those states which adopt truth-in-sentencing laws (violent offenders must serve at least 85% of their sentence) or which meet other conditions. $24.5 million in competitive funds available for boot camps in 1995. $7.9 billion authorized in 1996-2000.

DRUG COURTS

Competitive grant program to support state and local drug courts which provide supervision and specialized services to offenders with rehabilitation potential. $29 million available in 1995. $971 million authorized in 1996–2000.

FAMILY AND COMMUNITY ENDEAVOR SCHOOLS

Competitive grants program administered by the Department of Education for localities and community organizations to help improve the overall development of at-risk youth living in poor and high-crime communities. This program is for both in-school and after-school activities. $11 million available in 1995. $232 million authorized in 1996–2000.

HOTLINE

Competitive grant program administered by the Department of Health and Human Services to establish a National Domestic Violence Hotline. $1 million authorized in 1995. $2 million authorized in 1996–2000.

PREVENTION COUNCIL

Provides funding for the President's Prevention Council to coordinate new and existing crime prevention programs. $1.5 million available in 1995. $88.5 million authorized for competitive grants in 1996–2000.

SCAAP GRANTS

Formula grant program to reimburse states for the cost of incarcerating criminal aliens. $130 million available in 1995. $1.67 billion authorized in 1996–2000.

VIOLENCE AGAINST WOMEN

Formula grant program to support police and prosecutor efforts and victims services in cases involving sexual violence or domestic abuse, and for other programs which strengthen enforcement and provide services to victims in such cases. $26 million available in 1995. $774 million for formula grants and over $200 million for competitive grants authorized in 1996–2000.

GRANT PROGRAMS FOR 1996–2000

All programs available in 1995 are continued. All programs are administered by the Department of Justice unless otherwise noted. Funding for 1996–2000 is, as always, subject to appropriation by the Congress.

BATTERED WOMEN'S SHELTERS

Competitive grant program administered by the Department of Health and Human Services for battered women's shelters and other domestic violence prevention activities. $325 million authorized.

CAPITAL IMPROVEMENTS TO PREVENT CRIME IN PUBLIC PARKS

Competitive grant program administered by the Department of Interior for states and localities for crime prevention programs in national and public parks. $15 million authorized.

COMMUNITY ECONOMIC PARTNERSHIP

Competitive program administered by the Department of Health and Human Services for lines of credit to community development corporations to stimulate business and employment opportunities for low-income, unemployed and underemployed individuals. $270 million authorized.

CRIME PREVENTION BLOCK GRANTS

$377 million authorized for a new Local Crime Prevention Block Grant program to be distributed to local governments to be used as local needs dictates. Authorized programs include: anti-gang programs, sports leagues, boys and girls clubs, partnerships (triads) between the elderly and law enforcement, police partnerships for children and youth skills programs.

DELINQUENT AND AT-RISK-YOUTH

Competitive grant program for public or private nonprofit organizations to support the development and operation of projects to provide residential services to youth, aged 11 to 19, who have dropped out of school, have come into contact with the juvenile justice system or are at risk of either. $36 million authorized.

DNA ANALYSIS

Competitive grant program for states and localities to develop or improve DNA identification capabilities. $40 million authorized. An additional $25 million is authorized to the FBI for DNA identification programs.

DRUG TREATMENT

$383 million for prison drug treatment programs, including $270 million in formula grants for states.

EDUCATION AND PREVENTION TO REDUCE SEXUAL ASSAULTS AGAINST WOMEN

Competitive grant program administered by the Department of Health and Human Services to fund rape prevention and education programs in the form of educational seminars, hotlines, training programs for professionals and the preparation of informational materials. $205 million authorized.

LOCAL PARTNERSHIP ACT

Formula grant program administered by the Department of Housing and Urban Development for localities to enhance education, provide substance abuse treatment and fund job programs to prevent crimes. $1.6 billion authorized.

MODEL INTENSIVE GRANTS

Competitive grant program for model crime prevention programs targeted at high-crime neighborhoods. Up to 15 cities will be selected. $625 million authorized.

POLICE CORPS

Competitive funding for the Police Corps (college scholarships for students who agree to serve as police officers), and formula grants to states for scholarships to in-service law enforcement officers. $100 million authorized for Police Corps, and $100 million authorized for in-service law enforcement scholarships.

PROSECUTORS

Competitive grant program for state and local courts, prosecutors and public defenders. $150 million authorized.

RURAL LAW ENFORCEMENT

Formula grant program for rural anti-crime and drug enforcement efforts, including task forces. $240 million authorized.

TECHNICAL AUTOMATION

Competitive grant program to support technological improvements for law enforcement agencies and other activities to improve law enforcement training and information systems. $130 million authorized.

URBAN RECREATION FOR AT-RISK-YOUTH

Competitive grant program administered by the Department of Interior for localities to provide recreation facilities and services in areas with high crime rates and to provide such services in other areas to at-risk-youth. $4.5 million authorized.

October 24, 1994

DRAWING CONCLUSIONS:

1. How does this bill fuel the era of mass incarceration?
2. How does policing and incarceration become so racialized?
3. What does this bill provide police departments across the country?
4. What kinds of community-based support systems are offered by this bill?

THE MOVEMENT(S) CONTINUES

5.1   RODNEY KING (1991)

On March 3, 1991, Rodney King was severely beaten by Los Angeles police during his arrest, after a car chase. Prior to mobile digital technology, the home video recording of police beating King was a rare capturing of the police brutality Black and Latino communities had long protested. Police officers struck King over fifty times with batons, breaking his hand and severely bruising his face and body. The video and subsequent trial of the accused officers dominated the media for months. Hours after their acquittal, Los Angeles erupted in riots that lasted for six days.

GUIDING QUESTIONS:

1. Describe what is happening in this image.
2. What arguments would the police provide for needing to use force to detain and arrest King?

IMAGE 11 RODNEY KING IMAGE (1991)

DRAWING CONCLUSIONS:

1. Why is it important that citizens record police encounters?

2. What has been the impact of these recordings on policing?

From "Op-Ed: Rodney King's Beating Provides a Road Map of Investigating Police Misconduct," June 11, 2020, *Los Angeles Times*, https://www.latimes.com/opinion/story/2020-06-11/rodney-king-police-misconduct-investigations

5.2 MURDER OF TRAYVON MARTIN (IMAGE AND COMMENTARY)

The murder of Trayvon Martin became a centerpiece to the culture wars in the United States, amplifying racial discourse in the Obama era. Following is an excerpt from leading public intellectual Ta-Nehisi Coates in which he highlights this nexus between Martin's shooting and the nation's first Black president.

GUIDING QUESTIONS:

1. What does Coates say about President Obama's approach to public discussions regarding race?
2. Why did President Obama's comment about Trayvon Martin prompt a backlash from political opponents?

TA-NEHISI COATES, "FEAR OF A BLACK PRESIDENT" (2012) (EXCERPT)

As a candidate, Barack Obama said we needed to reckon with race and with America's original sin, slavery. But as our first black president, he has avoided mention of race almost entirely. In having to be "twice as good" and "half as black," Obama reveals the false promise and double standard of integration.

The irony of President Barack Obama is best captured in his comments on the death of Trayvon Martin, and the ensuing fray. Obama has pitched his presidency as a monument to moderation. He peppers his speeches with nods to ideas originally held by conservatives. He routinely cites Ronald Reagan. He effusively praises the enduring wisdom of the American people, and believes that the height of insight lies in the town square. Despite his sloganeering for change and progress, Obama is a conservative revolutionary, and nowhere is his conservative character revealed more than in the very sphere where he holds singular gravity—race.

Part of that conservatism about race has been reflected in his reticence: for most of his term in office,

Obama has declined to talk about the ways in which race complicates the American present and, in particular, his own presidency. But then, last February, George Zimmerman, a 28-year-old insurance underwriter, shot and killed a black teenager, Trayvon Martin, in Sanford, Florida. Zimmerman, armed with a 9 mm handgun, believed himself to be tracking the movements of a possible intruder. The possible intruder turned out to be a boy in a hoodie, bearing nothing but candy and iced tea. The local authorities at first declined to make an arrest, citing Zimmerman's claim of self-defense. Protests exploded nationally. Skittles and Arizona Iced Tea assumed totemic power. Celebrities—the actor Jamie Foxx, the former Michigan governor Jennifer Granholm, members of the Miami Heat—were photographed wearing hoodies. When Representative Bobby Rush of Chicago took to the House floor to denounce racial profiling, he was removed from the chamber after donning a hoodie mid-speech.

The reaction to the tragedy was, at first, transpartisan. Conservatives either said nothing or offered

Ta-Nehisi Coates, "Fear of a Black President," https://www.theatlantic.com/magazine/archive/2012/09/fear-of-a-black-president/309064/

Trayvon Martin, undated photos, accessed through *Los Angeles Times* article, "Sanford Police Chief Bill Lee fired after Trayvon Martin Case," June 20, 2012, https://www.latimes.com/nation/la-xpm-2012-jun-20-la-na-nn-sanford-police-chief-bill-lee-fired-20120620-story.html

tepid support for a full investigation—and in fact it was the Republican governor of Florida, Rick Scott, who appointed the special prosecutor who ultimately charged Zimmerman with second-degree murder. As civil-rights activists descended on Florida, National Review, a magazine that once opposed integration, ran a column proclaiming "Al Sharpton Is Right." The belief that a young man should be able to go to the store for Skittles and an iced tea and not be killed by a neighborhood-watch patroller seemed un-controversial.

By the time reporters began asking the White House for comment, the president likely had already given the matter considerable thought. Obama is not simply America's first black president—he is the first president who could credibly teach a black-studies class. He is fully versed in the works of Richard Wright and James Baldwin, Frederick Douglass and Malcolm X. Obama's two autobiographies are deeply concerned with race, and in front of black audiences he is apt to cite important but obscure political figures such as George Henry White, who served from 1897 to 1901 and was the last African American congressman to be elected from the South until 1970. But with just a few notable exceptions, the president had, for the first three years of his presidency, strenuously avoided talk of race. And yet, when Trayvon Martin died, talk Obama did:

> When I think about this boy, I think about my own kids, and I think every parent in America should be able to understand why it is absolutely imperative that we investigate every aspect of this, and that everybody pulls together—federal, state, and local—to figure out exactly how this tragedy happened ...
>
> But my main message is to the parents of Trayvon Martin. If I had a son, he'd look like Trayvon. I think they are right to expect that all of us as Americans are going to take this with the seriousness it deserves, and that we're going to get to the bottom of exactly what happened.

The moment Obama spoke, the case of Trayvon Martin passed out of its national-mourning phase and lapsed into something darker and more familiar—racialized political fodder. The illusion of consensus crumbled... .

The irony of Barack Obama is this: he has become the most successful black politician in American history by avoiding the radioactive racial issues of yesteryear, by being "clean" (as Joe Biden once labeled him)—and yet his indelible blackness irradiates everything he touches. This irony is rooted in the greater ironies of the country he leads. For most of American history, our political system was premised on two conflicting facts—one, an oft-stated love of democracy; the other, an undemocratic white supremacy inscribed at every level of government. In warring against that paradox, African Americans have historically been restricted to the realm of protest and agitation. But when President Barack Obama pledged to "get to the bottom of exactly what happened," he was not protesting or agitating. He was not appealing to federal power—he was employing it. The power was black—and, in certain quarters, was received as such ...

It is often said that Obama's presidency has given black parents the right to tell their kids with a straight face that they can do anything. This is a function not only of Obama's election to the White House but of the way his presidency broadcasts an easy, almost mystic, blackness to the world. The Obama family represents our ideal imagining of ourselves—an ideal we so rarely see on any kind of national stage.

What black people are experiencing right now is a kind of privilege previously withheld—seeing our most sacred cultural practices and tropes validated in the world's highest office. Throughout the whole of American history, this kind of cultural power was wielded solely by whites, and with such ubiquity that it was not even commented upon. The expansion of this cultural power beyond the private province of whites has been a tremendous advance for black America. Conversely, for those who've long treasured white exclusivity, the existence of a President Barack Obama is discombobulating, even terrifying. For as surely as the iconic picture of the young black boy reaching out to touch the president's curly hair sends one message to black America, it sends another to those who have enjoyed the power of whiteness.

Then the first black president spoke, and the Internet bloomed. Young people began "Trayvoning"—mocking the death of a black boy by photographing themselves in hoodies, with Skittles and iced tea, in a death pose.

In a democracy, so the saying goes, the people get the government they deserve. Part of Obama's genius

IMAGE 12 TRAYVON MARTIN

is a remarkable ability to soothe race consciousness among whites. Any black person who's worked in the professional world is well acquainted with this trick. But never has it been practiced at such a high level, and never have its limits been so obviously exposed. This need to talk in dulcet tones, to never be angry regardless of the offense, bespeaks a strange and compromised integration indeed, revealing a country so infantile that it can countenance white acceptance of blacks only when they meet an Al Roker standard.

DRAWING CONCLUSIONS:

1. What does the "hoodie" represent in our nation's culture wars?
2. What is Florida's "Stand Your Ground" law?
3. How did Trayvon Martin's murder inspire the Black Lives Matter movement?

5.3 THE MOVEMENT FOR BLACK LIVES, "VISION FOR BLACK LIVES" 2020 POLICY PLATFORM (2020)

The Movement for Black Lives emerged in direct response and opposition to police shootings of unarmed Black people. Anchored by a national coalition of local organizations, the movement has created a platform and broadly democratic structure to engage voices across the country. In this new millennium, the Movement for Black Lives highlights the persistence of racial inequality, and the sustained persistence of the Black Liberation Movement(s).

GUIDING QUESTIONS:

1. What issues are of concern to the Movement for Black Lives?
2. How are these contemporary challenges similar to or different from past ones?

VISION FOR BLACK LIVES

Black life and dignity require Black political will and power. Despite constant exploitation and perpetual oppression, Black people have bravely and brilliantly been a driving force pushing toward collective liberation. In recent years, we have taken to the streets, launched massive campaigns, and impacted elections, but our elected leaders have failed to address the legitimate demands of our Movement. We can no longer wait.

In response to the sustained and increasingly visible violence against Black communities in the U.S. and globally, a collective of more than 50 organizations representing thousands of Black people from across the country came together in 2015 with renewed energy and purpose to articulate a common vision and agenda. We are a collective that centers, and is led by and rooted in, Black communities. And we recognize our shared struggle with all oppressed people: collective liberation will be a product of all of our work.

We are intentional about amplifying the particular experiences of racial, economic, and gender-based state and interpersonal violence that Black women, queer, trans, gender nonconforming, intersex, and disabled people face. Cisheteropatriarchy and ableism are central and instrumental to anti-Blackness and racial capitalism, and have been internalized within our communities and movements.

The Movement for Black Lives (M4BL) launched the Vision for Black Lives, a comprehensive and visionary policy agenda for the post-Ferguson Black liberation movement, in August of 2016. The Vision, endorsed by over 50 Black-led organizations in the M4BL ecosystem and hundreds of allied organizations and individuals, has since inspired campaigns across the country to achieve its goals.

After three years of consultations, writing retreats and Zoom sessions, research and outreach, we are re-launching the Vision for Black Lives 2020. We will be rolling out revised, updated, and expanded policy briefs for each of the six planks of the platform over the coming months, leading up to a National Black Convention in August of 2020.

We begin with the first plank of our Vision: End the War on Black People, released on Juneteenth as we converge across the country in resistance to police and state sanctioned violence.

From The Movement for Black Lives, "Platform," https://m4bl.org/policy-platforms/

This document does not represent the entirety of our Vision – it is only the first section of six, and focuses on state violence. We will be re-releasing revised and expanded policy briefs in each of the remaining sections of the Vision – Reparations, Economic Justice, Invest/Divest, Community Control and Political Power – over the course of 2020

2020 POLICY PLATFORM

The Preamble

END THE WAR ON BLACK COMMUNITIES
END THE WAR ON BLACK YOUTH
END THE WAR ON BLACK WOMEN
END THE WAR ON BLACK TRANS, QUEER, GENDER NONCONFORMING AND INTERSEX PEOPLE
END THE WAR ON BLACK HEALTH AND BLACK DISABLED PEOPLE

END THE WAR ON BLACK MIGRANTS
END TO ALL JAILS, PRISONS, AND IMMIGRATION DETENTION
END THE DEATH PENALTY
END THE WAR ON DRUGS
END THE SURVEILLANCE ON BLACK COMMUNITIES
END TO PRETRIAL DETENTION AND MONEY BAIL
THE DEMILITARIZATION OF LAW ENFORCEMENT
END THE USE OF PAST CRIMINAL HISTORY

DRAWING CONCLUSIONS:

1. How does the movement's vision reflect long-standing issues around Black equality?
2. What "new" topics and voices are centered in the Movement for Black Lives?

5.4 MASS INCARCERATION AND FELON DISFRANCHISEMENT

The United States is the global leader in incarceration, which is furthered marred by significant racial disparities. One key outgrowth of mass incarceration is felon disfranchisement. The following fact sheet from the Roosevelt Institute highlights data on the numbers of people impacted by this policy trend, as well as potential solutions. (Note: Florida has recently amended its felon voting laws.)

GUIDING QUESTIONS:

1. What are some political outcomes associated with racial disparities in incarceration and felon disfranchisement?
2. What histories help to inform why felons lose their voting rights?

From Voting Rights Restoration Fact Sheet, Roosevelt Institute, https://rooseveltinstitute.org/wp-content/uploads/2016/09/RR_FactsheetV6.pdf

The Problem: Voter Disenfranchisement

The United States has the highest incarceration rate in the world with close to 2.2 million people behind bars. Studies have shown that changes in the criminal justice system and in sentencing laws, not changes in crime rates, are responsible for these shocking numbers. One of the hidden costs of the mass incarceration epidemic is the inability of people to exercise their constitutional right to vote.

- The number of people disenfranchised due to a felony conviction has increased dramatically in recent decades as the prison population has increased. There were an estimated 1.17 million people disenfranchised in 1976, 3.34 million in 1996, 5.85 million in 2010, and 6.1 million as of 2016. Without a drastic change in disenfranchisement law, population growth will continue to fuel this trend.

- Approximately 2.5 percent of the total U.S. voting age population—1 out of every 40 adults—is disenfranchised due to a current or previous felony conviction.

- Florida is one of only four states (along with South Dakota, Iowa, and Virginia) with a lifetime ban on voting for any person convicted of a felony. There are 1.5 million Florida residents that are unable to vote- 1 in 10 Floridians of voting age are disenfranchised.

- Nationally, more than 60 percent of those in prison today are people of color. One in 13 African Americans of voting age are disenfranchised, a rate more than four times greater than for non-African Americans.

The Solution: Rights Restoration

Felon disenfranchisement is a relic of the Jim Crow era. It was a policy that was meant to exclude African Americans from participating in civic institutions and the electoral process. Resulting in the rules being written to privilege some in society while stifling the voices of others. The only way for us to have a fair and inclusive democratic process is if we rewrite the very rules that were engineered against these citizens.

- Voting is a civic duty. It brings us together as Americans and helps strengthen our communities. Americans should have a say in their future, their children's futures, and the future of our great nation.

- When you have served your time, you should earn your rights back. Many taxpaying, law-abiding citizens who have completed their sentences are still unable to vote.

- Everyone deserves a second chance. Restoring a person's right to vote gives them an opportunity for redemption and a chance to reenter society as civically engaged community members.

- People who have served their time and given an opportunity to participate in the civic process are less likely to commit crimes in the future. A report by the Florida Parole Commission concluded that the three-year recidivism rate for all released inmates was 33.1 percent, while the recidivism rate for released prisoners who had their voting rights restored was only 11 percent.

Source: Uggen, Christopher, Ryan Larson, and Sarah Shannon. *6 Million Lost Voters: State-level Estimates of Felon Disenfranchisement, 2016*. Washington, D.C.: Sentencing Project, 2016. Print.

ROOSEVELTINSTITUTE.ORG

IMAGE 13 VOTING RIGHTS RESTORATION FACT SHEET, ROOSEVELT INSTITUTE

DRAWING CONCLUSIONS:

1. Should felons be denied the right to vote? If so, when should those rights be restored?

5.5 AMERICAN CIVIL LIBERTIES UNION (ACLU) STOP-AND-FRISK CASES (NEW YORK CITY AND MILWAUKEE)

Black communities have long complained about racialized policing. Overpolicing Black communities is the progeny of historical patterns used to maintain control over Black bodies, extending from racialized notions of African American criminality. The ACLU exposed recent inequities with policing by litigating stop-and-frisk cases in key cities across the country. Following are documents highlighting stop-and-frisk data and commentary from New York City and Milwaukee.

GUIDING QUESTIONS:

1. What do the data reveal about racialized policing in American cities?
2. What were the outcomes of ACLU litigation?

ACLU OF NEW YORK (NYCLU), 2002–2019

Annual Stop-and-Frisk Numbers:

An analysis by the NYCLU revealed that innocent New Yorkers have been subjected to police stops and street interrogations more than 5 million times since 2002, and that black and Latino communities continue to be the overwhelming target of these tactics. Nearly nine out of 10 stopped-and-frisked New Yorkers have been completely innocent.

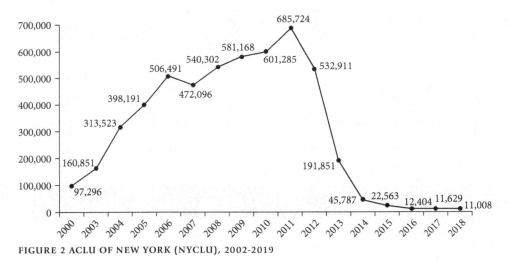

Number of reported NYPD stop-and-frisks 2002–2018

FIGURE 2 ACLU OF NEW YORK (NYCLU), 2002-2019

From ACLU of New York, Stop and Frisk Data, https://www.nyclu.org/en/stop-and-frisk-data; ACLU, *Collins et. al v. City of Milwaukee et al.*, https://www.aclu.org/cases/collins-et-al-v-city-milwaukee-et-al

(Select annual data sets from graph)

In 2002, 97,296 NYPD stops were recorded.
80,176 were innocent (82 percent).

In 2003, 160,851 NYPD stops were recorded.
140,442 were innocent (87 percent).
77,704 were black (54 percent).
44,581 were Latino (31 percent).
17,623 were white (12 percent).
83,499 were aged 14–24 (55 percent).

In 2011, 685,724 NYPD stops were recorded.
605,328 were innocent (88 percent).
350,743 were Black (53 percent).
223,740 were Latinx (34 percent).
61,805 were white (9 percent).
341,581 were aged 14–24 (51 percent).
(Lawsuit filed in 2012)
In the first quarter of 2019, 3,175 stops were recorded.
2,142 were innocent (68 percent).
1,900 were black (60 percent).
914 were Latino (29 percent).
290 were white (9 percent).

NYCLU's most recent detailed analysis of stop-and-frisk data and practices can be found in our 2019 report, "Stop-and-Frisk in the de Blasio Era."

About the Data:

Every time a police officer stops a person in NYC, the officer *is supposed to* fill out a form recording the details of the stop. The forms were filled out by hand and manually entered into an NYPD database until 2017, when the forms became electronic. The NYPD reports stop-and-frisk data in two ways: a summary report released quarterly and a complete database released annually to the public.

The quarterly reports are released by the NYCLU every three months [and] include data on stops, arrests, and summonses. The data are broken down by precinct of the stop and race and gender of the person stopped.

The annual database includes nearly all of the data recorded by the police officer after a stop such as the age of the person stopped, if a person was frisked, if there was a weapon or firearm recovered, if physical force was used, and the exact location of the stop within the precinct. The NYPD uploads this database to their website annually …

ACLU-WISCONSIN, 2007–2017

The American Civil Liberties Union, the ACLU of Wisconsin, and the law firm of Covington & Burling LLP filed a class-action lawsuit today against the City of Milwaukee over its police department's vast and unconstitutional stop-and-frisk program. The department targets tens of thousands of people without reasonable suspicion of criminal activity, the legal requirement for a police stop. The department's repeated violations of Milwaukeeans' constitutional rights are driven by racial profiling, with preliminary data showing significant disparities between police stop rates for white people and for Black and Latino people.

For almost a decade, the Milwaukee Police Department has pursued an aggressive and unconstitutional policing strategy promoting large numbers of stops and frisks citywide. Between 2007 and 2015, the department almost tripled their traffic and pedestrian stops, from around 66,000 to around 196,000, following the launch of the program in 2008.

Milwaukee residents have long protested that police officers are conducting stops and frisks of innocent people, and particularly treating people of color as suspects for no good reason, stopping innocent men, women, and children as they try to go about their daily lives. The department conducts far more stops and frisks in the parts of Milwaukee that are predominantly Black or Latino than in other areas.

In 2011, the Milwaukee Journal Sentinel found that Milwaukee police were seven times more likely to stop Black drivers than white drivers, and five times more likely to stop Hispanic drivers than white drivers. According to the ACLU's preliminary analysis of records from a Milwaukee police database on stops, Black (non-Hispanic) people were the targets of 72% of stops from 2010 through 2012 when they made up 34% of the city's total population, according to U.S. census figures.

The Milwaukee Police Department's unlawful stop-and-frisk program has caused the City's Black and Latino communities to feel alienated from the police, damaging the trust between police and the public central to achieving public safety. Black and Latino people throughout Milwaukee—including children—worry that they may be stopped, frisked, or otherwise treated like criminal suspects when doing nothing more than walking to a friend's house or home from school, driving to and from the homes of loved ones, running errands, or simply taking a leisurely walk or drive through the City.

Collins v. Milwaukee is brought by six people who are victims of the City's unlawful stop-and-frisk program on behalf of a class of similarly situated people. Each plaintiff is Black or Latino and was unlawfully stopped or unlawfully stopped and frisked on at least one occasion by Milwaukee police officers when engaged in routine activities, including walking home from school and driving home from a relative's house. The lawsuit brings a claim under the Fourth Amendment to the U.S. Constitution against the Milwaukee Police Department's practice of conducting stops without reasonable suspicion of criminal activity and frisks without reasonable suspicion that a person is armed and dangerous. It also brings claims under the Fourteenth Amendment and Title VI of the Civil Rights Act of 1964 against the Department's practice of stopping people based on their race or ethnicity.

Collins v. Milwaukee seeks an end to the Milwaukee Police Department's practice of conducting stops and frisks without reasonable suspicion, as well as its practice of stopping people based on their race or ethnicity. It also seeks reforms that safeguard constitutional rights by promoting bias-free and evidence-based policing, transparency, and police accountability. These reforms include improved training, supervision, and monitoring of officers who conduct stops and frisks, and the collection and semiannual release to the public of data on all stops and frisks to permit further analysis for evidence of constitutional violations.

On May 24, 2017, the Plaintiffs filed an amended complaint, adding three additional named plaintiffs to the lawsuit, one of whom is Rep. David Crowley, a state legislator representing Wisconsin's 17th Assembly District.

In July 2017 the parties reached a Settlement Agreement that was approved by Plaintiffs, the Common Council of the city of Milwaukee, and Mayor Tom Barrett. The parties filed a joint motion to the court for approval of the settlement agreement on July 13, 2017.

On July 23, 2017, the U.S. District Court for the Eastern District of Wisconsin entered an order adopting the Settlement Agreement. The agreement requires the Milwaukee Police Department and Milwaukee Fire and Police Commission to:

Change policies regarding stops and frisks;

Document every stop and every frisk conducted by officers, the reason for the encounter, and related demographic information, regardless of the outcome of the stop;

Improve training, supervision, and auditing of officers on stop and frisk and racial profiling issues, and provide for discipline of officers who conduct improper stops or fail to document those stops;

Release stop-and-frisk data regularly to the public;

Expand and improve the process for the public to file complaints against police officers;

Maintain the Milwaukee Community Collaborative Committee, which will seek community input policing strategies and their impact on the public to improve trust between law enforcement and city residents, and seek diverse representation on the committee; and

Use an independent consultant to evaluate whether the city, the police department, and the Fire and Police Commission are making sufficient progress in implementing the reforms and identifying and correcting unlawful stops and frisks.

The Settlement Agreement will remain in force for at least the next five years and is being monitored by Plaintiffs' counsel.

DRAWING CONCLUSIONS:

1. Will this litigation continue to stymie police harassment and overpolicing in general? Why or why not?
2. What elements of the Milwaukee settlement agreement seem most impactful for eradicating racialized policing practices?

5.6 NATIONAL ASSOCIATION FOR THE ADVANCEMENT OF COLORED PEOPLE (NAACP) FACT SHEET ON INCARCERATION, 2019

As the nation's leading civil rights organization, the NAACP continues to play a vital role in efforts to secure racial equality in the United States. This fact sheet on incarceration details the depths of the racial inequities in US jails and prisons.

GUIDING QUESTIONS:

1. What has led to the dramatic increase in incarceration in the United States?
2. How is the nation impacted by its reliance on incarceration?

CRIMINAL JUSTICE FACT SHEET

INCARCERATION TRENDS IN AMERICA

- Between 1980 and 2015, the number of people incarcerated in America increased from roughly 500,000 to over 2.2 million.
- Today, the United States makes up about 5% of the world's population and has 21% of the world's prisoners.
- 1 in every 37 adults in the United States, or 2.7% of the adult population, is under some form of correctional supervision.

RACIAL DISPARITIES IN INCARCERATION

- In 2014, African Americans constituted 2.3 million, or 34%, of the total 6.8 million correctional population.
- African Americans are incarcerated at more than 5 times the rate of whites.
- The imprisonment rate for African American women is twice that of white women.
- Nationwide, African American children represent 32% of children who are arrested, 42% of children who are detained, and 52% of children whose cases are judicially waived to criminal court.

- Though African Americans and Hispanics make up approximately 32% of the US population, they comprised 56% of all incarcerated people in 2015.
- If African Americans and Hispanics were incarcerated at the same rates as whites, prison and jail populations would decline by almost 40%.

DRUG SENTENCING DISPARITIES

- In the 2015 National Survey on Drug Use and Health, about 17 million whites and 4 million African Americans reported having used an illicit drug within the last month.
- African Americans and whites use drugs at similar rates, but the imprisonment rate of African Americans for drug charges is almost 6 times that of whites.
- African Americans represent 12.5% of illicit drug users, but 29% of those arrested for drug offenses and 33% of those incarcerated in state facilities for drug offenses.

EFFECTS OF INCARCERATION

- A criminal record can reduce the likelihood of a callback or job offer by nearly 50 percent. The negative impact of a criminal record is twice as large for African American applicants.

From NAACP Criminal Justice Fact Sheet, https://www.naacp.org/criminal-justice-fact-sheet/;
NAACP Fair Chance Hiring Fact Sheet, http://www.naacp.org/fairchancehiring/

- Infectious diseases are highly concentrated in corrections facilities: 15% of jail inmates and 22% of prisoners—compared to 5% of the general population—reported ever having tuberculosis, Hepatitis B and C, HIV/AIDS, or other STDs.
- In 2012 alone, the United States spent nearly $81 billion on corrections.
- Spending on prisons and jails has increased at triple the rate of spending on Pre-K-12 public education in the last thirty years.

FAIR CHANCE HIRING FACT SHEET

AT THE INTERSECTION OF RACE, THE CRIMINAL JUSTICE SYSTEM, AND EMPLOYMENT CRIMINAL JUSTICE

- Over 2.2 million individuals are in jail or prison in the United States.
- Approximately 95% of incarcerated individuals are eventually released into local communities nationwide.
- Nearly half of Black males and almost 40 percent of white males are arrested by the time they are 23 years old.
- As of 2007, more than half of those incarcerated were parents of children under the age of 18.
- The number of Americans with criminal records is about the same as the number of Americans with a 4-year degree.
- Although illicit drug use is approximately the same for African Americans as it is for white people, African Americans are much more likely to be arrested for drug use.

CRIMINAL RECORDS AND EMPLOYMENT

- Finding stable employment is crucial to ensuring that individuals do not reoffend.
- Having a record reduces the likelihood of a job callback or offer by as much as 50 percent.
- White men with a criminal record are more likely to get an interview than Black men with no criminal record.
- Reduced employment for the millions of people with records costs America $78 to $87 billion each year..

BAN THE BOX

- Ban the Box delays consideration of criminal records, but it does not prohibit employers from asking about criminal records later in the employment process.
- More than 25 states and 150 local areas have adopted Ban the Box laws and policies.
- In 9 states, Ban the Box laws apply to private employers.
- Studies on public sector Ban the Box laws and policies have found that Ban the Box increases opportunities for individuals with criminal records.

DRAWING CONCLUSIONS:

1. What data are most striking regarding incarceration?
2. How does incarceration limit life chances, post release?

5.7 EXPERTS OF COLOR NETWORK LETTER ON THE FLINT WATER CRISIS (2016)

Environmental racism is among the many direct outgrowths of the nation's history of residential segregation, and it is reflective of how the nation must grapple with the impact of decades of industrial production and waste. Access to fresh, clean water as a human right is increasingly becoming a very real issue in the United States, highlighted by the tragedy in Flint, Michigan, in 2014. The Flint Water Crisis occurred when local officials switched the region's water supply to the heavily contaminated Flint River from its previous sources of Lake Huron and the Detroit River, and failed to add important filtration systems. This letter by public health experts to the governor of Michigan highlights long-term individual, familial, and community impact of this human rights violation.

GUIDING QUESTIONS:
1. What caused the water crisis in Flint, Michigan?
2. Who is responsible for addressing this public health and human rights issue?

The Honorable Rick Snyder
Governor
State of Michigan
P.O. Box 30013
Lansing, MI 48909

As a coalition of more than 200 experts who are focused on building wealth for communities of color, we believe that it is vital for all public leaders in the U.S. to commit to advancing an inclusive democracy that fairly treats and affirms the value of all of its diverse residents. We have a number of concerns about the governance and water crisis in Flint, as well as some recommendations for remediation and change.

Our perspective is embedded in Article I of the Constitution of Michigan, which you have sworn to uphold, which states:

All power is inherent in the people. Government is instituted for their equal benefit, security and protection. No person shall be denied the equal protection of the laws; nor shall any person be denied the enjoyment of his civil or political rights or be discriminated against in the exercise

thereof because of religion, race, color or national origin … *The people have the right peaceably to assemble, to consult for the common good, to instruct their representatives and to petition the government for redress of grievances.[i]*

Based on the criteria established by Michigan's constitution and embedded in other state laws, it is reasonable to conclude that rights of the residents of Flint, MI have been abrogated. The people of Flint have not received equal benefit, security or protection from their government. They have been denied equal protection of the laws and seemingly discriminated against because of class and race. Their right to petition government for redress of grievances has also been obstructed.

We base these conclusions on the following facts:

- The emergency management law, passed with your support under the cover of expediency, gave your Administration the right to appoint an unelected overseer to manage the government of Flint. When your emergency manager decided to switch to a contaminated water source he endangered the

From Center for Global Policy Solutions, "Read the Experts of Color Network Letter on the Flint Water Crisis," http://globalpolicysolutions.org/read-experts-ofcolor-letter-on-flint/

health of tens of thousands of children, women, and men and damaged property.

- Scientists have analyzed differences in pediatric elevated blood lead level incidence before and after the water source change in Flint and have found that blood lead levels increased after the switch and that the incidence was greatest in socioeconomically disadvantaged areas of the city with high percentages of racial and ethnic minorities.[ii]
- The water in Flint also was filled with excessive levels of iron, copper and trihalomethanes, which present humans with a variety of other potential health risks. The chemicals were also responsible for the abnormal taste, look and smell of Flint's water. [iii]
- It has been documented that repeated attempts by these residents to seek redress for their grievances were met with scorn, dismissal, and contempt by your Administration's representatives.

In addition to damaging the health of Flint residents, we contend that your Administration's actions have also undermined their potential for maximizing earnings and accumulating wealth over a lifetime, which has a direct impact on the social and economic viability of the communities in which they reside.

Scientific evidence has long shown the devastating long-term effects of lead poisoning on the socioeconomic outcomes of exposed persons. Negative side effects include reproductive, neurophysiological, and behavioral disorders that can lead to toxic pregnancies, lower IQ, poor academic performance, and aggressive or violent behavior among other problems.[iv] The developmental effects are especially acute in children whose growing minds and bodies are severely compromised by lead poisoning.

When these side effects are visited upon a class of people concentrated in a geographic area, in many cases forced by socioeconomic circumstances to live in older neighborhoods with neglected infrastructure, the systemic conditions are created for failing schools, long term unemployment, increased poverty, high incarceration rates, lower tax receipts, and higher housing vacancy rates among other ills.

The water crisis has already stripped the assets of residents who have been forced to pay out of pocket for bottled water and for unusable city water. It will

also have long-term and negative effects on property values, which will depress homeowners' ability to accumulate wealth through their home equity. Since home equity is the primary vehicle through which many working families build wealth and save for retirement, property devaluations are likely to have a negative effect on their ability to maximize their economic security for the rest of their lives.

Ultimately, these man-made conditions make it near impossible for affected individuals to succeed in life or for our coalition to achieve our goal of building assets and economic security over a lifetime for vulnerable populations.

For these and related reasons we call upon you to exhibit transformational leadership that transcends the boundaries of bias, blame, thrift, and partisanship to embrace a fair and inclusive agenda for restoring hope and opportunity for the people of Flint. The remedies include:

- **Language:** Reports have shown that undocumented immigrants have been slow to receive word about Flint's water problems and that language barriers have interfered with their ability to seek appropriate testing and care. Additionally, the fear caused by Immigration and Custom Enforcement raids is further imperiling the health status of this population by impeding their ability to access free bottled water. We call on you to remove barriers to aid and assistance by ensuring that all announcements are bilingual and that trusted community members conduct Spanish language outreach to provide this vulnerable group with critical information. Furthermore, we call on you to request that ICE suspend raids in Flint given the city's ongoing humanitarian crises.
- **Compensation:** It is clear that, in addition to compromising resident's health and damaging their property and city infrastructure, Flint's water contamination will have long-term psychosocial and socioeconomic effects for individuals and families. We call on you to establish a Flint Health and Compensation Fund, modeled after the September 11 Victim Compensation Fund, to improve protection and services to individuals directly impacted by the water crisis. In addition to financing claims of those affected by the crisis, this fund would

cover the cost of health evaluation screenings for eligible residents, monitoring and treatment for related health conditions (without deductibles, co-payments, or other cost sharing), research regarding health and socioeconomic conditions related to the crisis, education and outreach to potentially eligible individuals. Since there is an arguable federal component to the Flint crisis, given long standing partisan gridlock that has denied states adequate federal infrastructure funding, we ask that you also lend the full weight of your authority and credibility toward establishing a federal version of, or contribution to, the fund.

- **Homeowner Relief:** The real estate market in Flint has been destabilized, with fewer people likely to buy homes in the city because of the market uncertainty associated with property damage caused by the water crisis and outstanding questions about the quality of the city's infrastructure The entire water system will likely need to be replaced in order to restore the natural real estate market in Flint. Based on the facts, the state needs to provide homeowners with relief that includes, but may not be limited to, writing off existing debt and tax liability on all affected properties.

- **Infrastructure:** For too long partisan gridlock at the federal and state levels has prevented states like Michigan from making the investments necessary to ensure the safety and protection of its residents. A recent study by the American Society of Civil Engineers gave Michigan a grade of D for the state of its infrastructure in general, as well as a D for the state of its drinking water more specifically[v]. We call on you to be a part of the solution by implementing a state infrastructure program, and advocating for a national infrastructure program, that modernizes aging infrastructure—starting in most affected areas—while creating jobs that benefit disadvantaged persons living in depressed areas like Flint, MI.

- **Regulation:** Partisan ideology has long pushed the notion that regulation stifles economic development and growth but situations like Flint demonstrate how loose regulations can compromise economic development by polluting public assets and damaging lives and property in the process. Flint's overseer sought to save the city $5 million by

switching to a harmful water source, yet the city and state will eventually incur millions more in associated costs to mitigate the damage caused by that ill-fated decision. The time is now to demonstrate good stewardship over the commonwealth by protecting these resources with sensible regulations.

- **Taxes:** Real fiscal prudence would suggest that it is never a good idea to reduce the tax base when there are obvious needs a government must address. Taxes are designed to ensure that government has the resources to provide for the common goods and services that people have determined they want and need for the betterment of society. Bestowing tax cuts and breaks—especially those benefitting culpable industries—while roads, bridges, and schools need repair, pipes need replacing, and water needs cleaning is the height of fiscal irresponsibility and malfeasance. Residents of Flint pay taxes to the state and it is important to ensure the equitable and responsible distribution of those taxes so that they are not unduly burdened by preventable crises like the one at hand. We call on you to suspend all tax cuts and breaks until the dire infrastructure needs of Michigan's most affected areas are met and to reassess priorities for distributing existing resources so that the needs of those who have been denied equal protection under the law can be addressed expeditiously.

There comes a time in the history of a state and our nation when the pettiness of our politics must give way to the greatness of our common humanity. That time is now. The people of Flint deserve the utmost consideration from state officials who are the custodians of their collective wellbeing. We know that you and your colleagues in the state of Michigan are up to the task, and we are willing to work with you to restore health, hope, and opportunity for the people of Flint.

DRAWING CONCLUSIONS:

1. In 2014 or 2015, would you drink, bathe, or prepare food with water in Flint, Michigan?
2. What would you do if you had no other alternatives to get fresh, clean water?
3. What are the long-term implications of the Flint Water Crisis?

5.8 PROTESTS IN RESPONSE TO POLICE KILLINGS OF BREONNA TAYLOR AND GEORGE FLOYD (2020)

The May 25, 2020, video recording of Minneapolis police officer Derek Chauvin killing George Floyd gained widespread attention as Black communities and activist groups learned more details about the Louisville police department's killing of Breonna Taylor on March 13, 2020. Less than one month prior to Taylor's murder on February 23, Ahmaud Abery was killed by three white men, and it was discovered that local authorities attempted to protect the killers from arrest and prosecution. Amid the COVID-19 pandemic, millions of people are taking part in continued demonstrations against police brutality, anti-Black racism, and White supremacy more broadly. Key threads to this upsurge in activism are calls to value, protect, and center the voices of Black women and queer Black people.

GUIDING QUESTIONS:

1. Note the sources for these images, and consider the local, national, and international implications of police killings and the ensuing protests.
2. Describe the images and discuss the protestors, the police, and their clothing and uniforms.
3. Connect these images to the Movement for Black Lives' "Vision for Black Lives" and "2020 Policy Platform.". Do the images help us better understand the demands?

IMAGE 14A GEORGE FLOYD

IMAGE 14B BREONNA TAYLOR

Siviwe Breakfast, "George Floyd Killing Opened Old Wounds for SA, Says Ramaphosa," June 6, 2020, *The South African*, https://www.thesouthafrican.com/news/george-floyd-killing-opened-old-wounds-for-sa-says-ramaphosa/

Whitney Curtis, "Here's What You Need to Know about Breonna Taylor's Death," September 5, 2020, *The New York Times*, https://www.nytimes.com/article/breonna-taylor-police.html

Richard A. Oppel Jr., Derrick Bryson Taylor, and Nicholas Bogel-Burroughs, "What We Know about Breonna Taylor's Case and Death," October 2, 2020, *The New York Times*, https://www.nytimes.com/article/breonna-taylor-police.html

IMAGE 14C PROTESTORS

DRAWING CONCLUSIONS:

1. Will this upsurge in the Black Liberation Movement(s) lead to substantive change? Why or why not?
2. Why are politicians and local law enforcement resistant to current demands to divest from police and invest in local community-based strategies, but have always welcomed more militarized policing?
3. Discuss how the Movement for Black Lives is evolving?

For additional digital learning resources, please go to https://www.oup.com/he/smith1e

ADDITIONAL RESOURCES

Alexander, Michelle. *The New Jim Crow: Mass Incarceration in the Age of Colorblindness*. New York: New Press. Distributed by Perseus Distribution, 2010.

Baldwin, James. *Notes of a Native Son*. New York: Beacon Press, 2012.

Bell, Derrick. *Faces at the Bottom of the Well: The Permanence of Racism*. New York: Basic Book, 2008.

Berg, Manfred. *"The Ticket to Freedom": The NAACP and the Struggle for Black Political Integration*. Gainesville: University Press of Florida, 2005.

Cha-Jua, Sundiata Keita, and Clarence Long. "The 'Long Movement' as Vampire: Temporal and Spatial Fallacies in Recent Black Freedom Studies." *The Journal of African American History 92*, no. 2 (Spring 2007): 265–288.

Dowd Hall, Jacquelyn. "The Long Civil Rights Movement and the Political Uses of the Past." *Journal of American History 91*, no. 4 (March 2005): 1233–1263.

Foner, Eric, and Joshua Brown. *Forever Free: The Story of Emancipation and Reconstruction*. New York: Knopf, 2006.

Hinton, Elizabeth. *From the War on Poverty to the War on Crime: The Making of Mass Incarceration in America*. Cambridge, MA: Harvard University Press, 2016.

Lichtenstein, Alex. *Twice the Work of Free Labor: The Political Economy of Convict Labor in the New South*. New York: Verso, 1996.

Lipsitz, George. *The Possessive Investment in Whiteness: How White People Profit from Identity Politics*. Philadelphia: Temple University Press, 1998.

Muhammad, Kahlil. *The Condemnation of Blackness: Race, Crime, and the Making of Modern Urban America*. Cambridge, MA: Harvard University Press, 2010.

Musgrove, George Derek. *Rumor, Repression, and Racial Politics: How the Harassment of Black Elected Officials Shaped Post–Civil Rights America*. Athens: University of Georgia Press, 2012.

Ransby, Barbara. *Ella Baker and the Black Freedom Movement: A Radical Democratic Vision*. Chapel Hill: The University of North Carolina Press, 2005.

Rothstein, Richard. *The Color of Law: A Forgotten History of How Our Government Segregated America*. New York: Liveright, 2017.

Sugrue, Thomas. *Sweet Land of Liberty: The Forgotten Struggle for Civil Rights in the North*. New York: Random House, 2009.

Trotter, Joe William. *Black Milwaukee: The Making of an Industrial Proletariat, 1915–45*. 2nd ed. Urbana: University of Illinois Press, 2007.

INDEX

Note: Page numbers followed by *f* indicate a figure on the corresponding page.

the Regulators, 57
religious organizations, 11
reparations, 62–63
Republican Party, 12, 30
residential segregation, 64–65
restrictive covenants and Jim Crow, 64–65
Roberson, Willie, 60
Roosevelt, Franklin D., 114–115
Roosevelt Institute, 142, 143*f*
rural law enforcement grants in Clinton Crime
    Bill, 133
Rush, Bobby, 137
Rustin, Bayard, 4

Sanchez, Sonia, 28
Santa Clara County jail, 108
SCAAP grants in Clinton Crime Bill, 132
school-to-prison pipeline, 33
Scott, Rick, 138
Scottsboro Case (1930s), 9–10, 60–61, 60*f*
Second Reconstruction, 10
segregation; Civil Rights Act of 1875 and,
    7, 14, 45–46, 123; desegregation of
    K-12 education, 32; Jim Crow era, 5, 30,
    91; legitimization of, 7, 15; residential
    segregation, 64–65
self-dependence, 82
self-expression, 82, 83
self-identity, 8
self-respect, 72, 82
sexism within civil rights leadership, 100
sex offender imprisonment in Clinton Crime
    Bill, 131
sex offender registration in Clinton Crime Bill,
    131
sharecropping in Jim Crow era, 7, 52–54
Shaw University, 100
Shelley v. *Kraemer* (1948), 10, 117
Sipuel v. *Board of Regents* (1948), 117
sit-inners, 27
slavery; abolition of, 5, 6; continued impact
    of, 38–39; emancipation and, 56–57; Jim
    Crow and, 7
Social Darwinists, 6
social equality, 76
Soledad Prison, 108
Some "Dont's" (*Chicago Defender*), 72–73

Southern Christian Leadership Conference
    (SCLC), 18, 108
Southern Democrats (Dixiecrats), 26, 30
Southern Manifesto, 26
"Speech at Howard University" (Chisolm),
    104–106
"Speech Delivered at the Embassy Auditorium"
    (Davis), 107–110
spiritual emancipation, 82
state violence, 3, 33, 141
stop-and-frisk cases, 144–146, 144*f*
"Strange Fruit" (song), 84
Student Nonviolent Coordinating Committee
    (SNCC), 18, 19, 100, 108
suffrage movement, 56
Survey Graphic, 81
Sweatt v. Painter (1950), 116–118
systemic racism, 12

Taylor, Breonna, 10, 21, 152–153, 152*f*, 153*f*
technical automation grants in Clinton Crime
    Bill, 134
Thirteenth Amendment (US Constitution),
    6, 14, 38
three strikes clause in Clinton Crime Bill, 131
Title VII litigation, 31
trans women of color, 11
Trump, Donald, 11–12, 20, 34
Tulsa Massacre (1921), 8
Tuskegee Health Benefit Program (THBP), 63
"Tuskegee Study of Untreated Syphilis in the
    Negro Male," 62–63
Twenty-Fourth Amendment
    (US Constitution), 128
Twenty-Sixth Amendment (US Constitution), 128

Universal Negro Improvement Association
    (UNIA), 9, 16, 75–77
University of Texas Law School, 116–117
urbanization of Black America, 8–10
Urban League, 9
urban recreation grants in Clinton Crime Bill, 134
urban renewal programs, 33, 69, 69*f*

Vietnam War, 27
violence against women in Clinton Crime
    Bill, 132